SPEEDWAY
THE GREATEST MOMENTS

BY THE SAME AUTHORS

JOHN CHAPLIN

Wings And Space: the History Of Aviation

Speedway: The Story Of The World Championship

John Chaplin's Speedway Special: The Classic Legends

Ove Fundin Speedway Superstar

Tom Farndon: The Greatest Speedway Rider Of Them All
(With Norman Jacobs)

Ivan Mauger: The Man Behind The Myth

Speedway Superheroes *(with John Somerville)*

Main Dane: My Story By Hans Nielsen
(Edit, production, design)

History Of The Speedway Hoskins By Ian Hoskins
(Edit, production, design)

A Fistful Of Twistgrip

Vintage Speedway Magazine
(Founder, Editor, Publisher)

JOHN SOMERVILLE

Speedway Times Past

The Illustrated History Of 100 British Speedway Tracks
(Both with Howard Jones)

Kiwi Kings Of Speedway

Speedway Superheroes *(with John Chaplin)*

SPEEDWAY
THE GREATEST MOMENTS

CHAPLIN AND SOMERVILLE

HALSGROVE

First published in Great Britain in 2014
Copyright © John Chaplin and John Somerville 2014

A CIP record for this title is available from the British Library

ISBN 978 0 85704 201 9

HALSGROVE
Halsgrove House,
Ryelands Business Park,
Bagley Road, Wellington, Somerset TA21 9PZ
Tel: 01823 653777   Fax: 01823 216796
email: sales@halsgrove.com

Part of the Halsgrove group of companies.
Information on all Halsgrove titles is available at: www.halsgrove.com

Printed in China by Everbest Printing Co Ltd

CONTENTS

AUTHORS' NOTE 6

FOREWORD 7

1. THRILLING THE WORLD 9

2. BUM'S THE WORD 15

3. THE REG & WALLY SHOW 16

4. AKKO'S EPIC NIGHT 26

5. THE INCREDIBLE PARKERS 30

6. TERMITE'S TRAVELS 47

7. PEERLESS PLECHANOV 50

8. YOUNG AUB AND HIS MYSTERY CHAPERONE 57

9. TRIUMPH AND TRAGEDY 64

10. MEET THE MASTERS 73

11. JACK MILNE'S THUMB 80

12. A BOY FROM BALHAM 86

13. DAYDREAM BELIEVER 94

14. THE 'RED HOT REXTON' RACING SENSATION 95

15. SAINT SPLIT 103

16. THE SECRET LIFE OF BASIL STOREY 116

17. TOP GUNS 122

18. CAPTAIN AMERICA 124

19. THE SECOND NOEL 131

20. MIRACLE AT THE ZOO 133

21. THE SENSATIONAL STENNERS 135

22. BY GEORGE ... IT'S THE HOUNDS 140

23. CACKLE 142

24. THE BOMBSHELL 144

25. SPEEDWAY'S CHAMPION THUNDER-STEALER 153

AUTHORS' NOTE

OUR first *Speedway Superheroes* book was so well received that our publisher, suggested we do another.

So we have.

And this is a collection of our favourite speedway pictures, and favourite speedway stories . . . the overwhelming majority of which are true.

John Chaplin and John Somerville

FOREWORD

JOHN CHAPLIN specializes in bringing speedway's past and its heroes back to life.

From his early beginnings as a schoolboy Birmingham fan in 1946, John has become the foremost authority on speedway (and dirt-track) history, hence his founding of the *Vintage Speedway Magazine* in 1993 along with fellow historian Peter Lipscomb.

The magazine, featuring stories and photographs from our sport's bygone days, was a great success and led to the launching of the annual High Beech reunions in February 1995 which celebrated the birth of dirt-track racing there in February 1928. This pre-season get-together proved very popular and outgrew the King's Oak Hotel and is now held at Paradise Wildlife Park each February.

John's stories about our sport's history have been published all over the speedway world, from *Speedway Star* in the UK to magazines in Sweden, California and Peter White's *Australian Speedway World* plus books on personalities such as Ove Fundin, Ivan Mauger, Hans Nielsen, Tom Farndon and Johnnie and Ian Hoskins.

So enjoy this latest book from the quill pen of speedway's leading historian.

Bert Harkins
Captain Wembley Lions 1971
President World Speedway Riders Assocation 2011

Also: London Match Race Champion 1971 (beat Benga Jansson at Wembley!); Captain of Edinburgh Monarchs 1977; Victorian Champion (Australia, not Queen!) 1967/68; South African Champion; Scottish Champion; Scotland Team Manager (but we don't have a team now); I forgot to mention World Best Pairs Finalist (Scotland with Jimmy Mac) Malmo, Sweden, 1971.

THE SOMERVILLE LEGACY

A FEW years ago I contacted my local paper in order to obtain a photograph that they had published in the 1980s. Being a sports photo and one taken at an international event, I felt confident that they'd either still have it on file, or knew the photographer so I could obtain it directly. I was shocked to learn that they had dumped the lot in a skip when they had been bought out by a larger publisher and gone completely digital. Since then I ve heard of similar stories, not only from the offices of periodical publications, but also relatives of deceased snappers who think such things have no value and have thrown them away.

From his base in Scotland, John Somerville has raced to the rescue, saving what he can from destruction and securing others for future generations to enjoy. But it's not been as simple as that because these collections come pretty much as they are; John's had to apply new technology to the old formats, such as glass plate negatives, slides, film negatives of all sizes as well as the more manageable modern digital format, to save the sport's visual record and make it accessible. Of course, some come in a disorganised manner to say the least, which makes you wonder how photographers operated as successfully as they did when seemingly applying such a chaotic method of storage. And then there is the legal side to it, the copyright issue, a complex law that's often open to widespread abuse.

Vitally important is the question of identification. Although an Edinburgh Monarchs supporter of long standing, John's knowledge doesn't and could not extend across the whole spectrum of speedway's near ninety-year history. Fortunately, he's able to call on a small army of enthusiasts whose knowledge of the sport's racers and administrators is such that they can identify an individual by the type of handlebars he used, the particular way a racer would bend his leg when cornering and, in the latter era, a sponsor's logo that appears on the rider's leathers.

The result is this vast collection – which now numbers in excess of one million images

– that covers the sport's formative years all the way up to the modern era. It includes the work of some of the sport's best-known photographers such as Wright Wood, Alf Weedon, Trevor Meeks and Mike Patrick, and a few less celebrated names that help make it perhaps the most comprehensive speedway photographic archive in the world.

His commitment and dedication in saving part of the sport's history is beyond admirable, it's damned-right inspiring because, without the likes of John Somerville to preserve this part of the sport, not only could the images be lost but also part of the sport's rich history with it. How many riders have taken to the track in British speedway since league racing started in 1929? Hundreds of thousands for sure, many of whom only spent a brief time competing before they disappeared, yet the chances are that you'll find that obscure rider who rode at number seven in a vital meeting in John's collection. Therefore, no longer is this person just a name in a match report, he now has a face, a personality and he mattered. That's how important John Somerville's archive is to the sport's history; its visual representation is not only a record of days gone by it also helps maintain its life and soul.

I'm sure you'll agree that the photos contained within this book, some historically important, some less so, all have a story to tell, a story that will be given more scope by John Chaplin's words. Pulitzer Prize-winning author, Eudora Welty (*The Optimist s Daughter*, 1972), once said that a good snapshot stops a moment from running away. Even without a camera, John Somerville has managed to do that and much, much more.

Brian Burford

Chapter 1
THRILLING THE WORLD

A. J. Hunting, the global colossus
. . . but JUST WHO DID 'invent' speedway?

WITHOUT a shadow of doubt we have to thank the Australians for putting speedway racing on the map in this country. The brilliant band of riders who came to England under the banner of Brisbane promoter A.J.Hunting, showed us that even the best Englishman was a raw novice. We did not know what broadsiding was until Huxley, Arthur and their colleagues dumbfounded the critics and crowds alike by seemingly laying their machines at impossible angles to send the cinders spouting Vesuvius-like from flying wheels over the fence and into the stands.

Tom Stenner, Thrilling The Million 1934

THE Old Warhorse, Johnnie S. Hoskins, invented speedway. Ever since Hoskins's Madcap Heroes first rode at Maitland's Hunter River Agricultural Showground in 1923, that is the legend that has persisted for 90 years.

But did he? Was his account true?

Johnnie's son Ian, himself a distinguished speedway promoter in his own right, has down the decades vociferously defended his parent as the Founding Father of speedway and jealously supported the claim against all-comers.

Yet there are some people who say that Johnnie's rival, A.J. Hunting, was really the man who started it all and did more to further the emergence of speedway into a recognised legitimate global mass sporting entertainment.

In the driving seat: A. J. Hunting.

Indeed, there is some anecdotal evidence to suggest that Mrs Hunting was the first person to use the term 'speedway'. Though, of course, there is almost certainly likely to be protracted verbal fisticuffs over that as well.

According to legend, in 1925 Mrs Hunting was so frustrated with her husband's motor racing projects, that she declared in a fit of fury: 'Our lives are full of that, that, that, that, that, speed . . . speed, speed, speed, speed . . . way!' A.J. then took the word Speedway for his companies.

The man himself certainly had no reservations about the origin of the world's most exciting sport. In a long-gone publication entitled *Answers*, dated 8 September 1928, under the subheading: *Thrilling The World*, there is the arresting proclamation HOW I INVENTED DIRT-TRACK RACING By A.J.Hunting, Managing Director of International Speedways Ltd.

By way of an introduction, a paragraph under the main headline reveals: 'A good dirt-track racer can earn £2,000 a year – and a number of English riders are now breaking into the game. In this article Mr Hunting prophesies dirt-track "Test Matches" between England and Australia, and tells for the first time the romantic story of how he invented the new sport which has taken the world by storm.'

You should know that the publication *Answers*, price one penny, was the forerunner of what is now called a tabloid newspaper and was launched by Fleet Street baron Alfred Harmsworth, the father of modern popular journalism, and later my employer Lord Northcliffe.

Answers was probably the original Penny Dreadful – a bit of a scandal sheet. Its jokes were known as 'genuine false-teeth looseners' and the stories relied heavily on the 'sharp wit and glorious imagination' of the founder.

Make of that what you will.

At first glance, the Hunting assertion that he invented dirt-track racing was rather like saying it was he and not Charles Lindbergh who was the first to fly the Atlantic solo, or that it was not Neil Armstrong who was the first human being to set foot on the Moon, but A. J. Hunting.

However, in fairness, A. J. deserves to have his say. Are you sitting comfortably? Then we'll let him begin:

'ALTHOUGH it is but three months since I introduced dirt-track racing to England, the sport has become firmly established over here. The thrills it produces – thrills which cannot be equalled by any other sport – have gripped the public, as I always believed they would, and huge crowds are turning up at our tracks.

Dirt-track racing sent my own country, Australia, into raptures, then captivated Britain, and is now repeating its triumphs in various other parts of the world. How did it all start? How did I get the idea of dirt-track racing and foster the sport until it became the big thing it is today? I will do my best to tell you.

About four years ago a friend gave me a ticket for a motorcycle race meeting on a grass track. I had never been to such a meeting before, and I went out of curiosity. It had been raining, and as soon as I arrived it was announced that the grass was too wet for racing. The management decided the races would be held on a cinder track which adjoined the grass one.

This was done and soon the whole crowd was on its feet, wild with excitement, for here was something new. Instead of slowing down to go round corners as was usual the riders were maintaining their speed and skidding round, giving us thrill after thrill as they righted their machines after it seemed as if crashes were imminent.

There and then I decided there was a big future for this sort of racing and I was soon making plans to build other cinder tracks in other parts of Australia. But before the afternoon was over there was a fatal accident . . . That made me give up the cinder track idea. I needed no further proof that it was far too dangerous. But the speed bug had got me . . .

The solution was to build a track with some substance like cinders which would make that wonderful broadsiding possible and would at the same time be a good deal safer for the riders.

I determined to get hold of this substance myself . . . and made experiments with various different kinds of earth until I produced the 'dirt' which is now used. Then I built the world's first dirt track at Brisbane.

When it was nearing completion I set the town ablaze with posters advertising the opening of the track and the birth of a great new sport. But what a job I had to find riders . . . willing to give dirt-track a chance.

Almost in despair I went to the Brisbane Motorcycling Club and pleaded for volunteers. At last a young man came forward . . . his name was Frank Pearce, now one of the finest dirt-track riders in the world. Charlie Spinks, then a bricklayer, was next to join me, and after him Vic Huxley. When the first meeting took place I had exactly 12 riders.

The crowd was just as enthusiastic as the crowd had been at that original cinder track. Soon letters came in from other motorcyclists anxious to ride while the crowds increased with each meeting. Other tracks were built all over Australia. The leading dirt-track riders became public idols and races for the sport's big trophies were followed with enormous interest.

It has been just the same over here. I have brought all my best riders from Australia with me and the English crowds have flocked to the tracks once the news of their skill and daring got round. Just to show how popular these riders are, let me tell you that such men as Cyclone Billy Lamont, Frank Arthur and Vic Huxley have already had hundreds of autograph albums sent to them to be signed.

Now a good man can earn as much as £2,000 a year. Frank Arthur has received more than £1,000 for an hour's actual riding, Vic Huxley has been getting as much. An Englishman, 'Smiling' Jim Kempster has earned £800 in the same time. These English riders have been showing remarkable promise in the game.

Kempster himself was the veriest novice a few weeks back. Jack Parker, Reg Pointer and Eric Spencer, other Englishmen who have not been riding long, can now hold their own with the best. I am quite sure that soon Test matches will be held between England and Australia at dirt-track racing. Indeed, the time is not far off when every town will have its dirt-track and a league championship will be fought for as in football.'

Master of ceremonies: Hunting, far left with the hat, at Brisbane Exhibition Speedway's third meeting on 14 November 1927.

***

WHAT a remarkable document. But before we examine it, we should know a little more about this man Hunting.

Australian historian Tony Webb, approved by the Hunting family as their archivist and biographer, who has conducted extensive research into Hunting's life for his book *Speedway Tonight: The Story Of Davies Park Speedway*, describes A.J. as a man before his time.

Albert John Hunting, says Webb, was a developer, speedway promoter, artist, visionary, dreamer, inventor, writer, commentator, thinker, farmer, writer and entrepreneur.

Before speedway this man of many parts had been a gold miner, farmer, baker, a Christmas stocking manufacturer, a poultry farmer and the designer of a waste paper recycling system. His original vision was to establish Brooklands-style motordromes in all Australian cities.

But, says Webb, his main claim to fame was as the man who took dirt-track racing, honed it into a professional entertainment and with his corporate expertise presented it to the world.

The assumptions in A.J.'s *Answers* article are staggering. When I first came across it I was struck by what appears to me to be monumental egotism glinting from every line. But under close scrutiny of the claims it gives itself away.

The clue is in the third paragraph. Remember the article is dated September 1928. In paragraph three A.J. states: 'About four years ago a friend in Sydney gave me a ticket for a motorcycle meeting on a grass track. I had never been to such a meeting before, and I went out of curiosity.'

'*About four years ago* . . . ' If calculated by the date on Mr Hunting's declared public pronouncements, that would mean 1924, would it not? Very well then, how does he explain this passage from my well-thumbed 1930 edition of *Roarin' Round The Speedways* by John S. Hoskins? On page six, under the heading 'How It All Started' we find the following: 'The idea was not new. There had been motorcycle racing one way and another from the day bikes first left the factory, but racing on small cinder tracks was indeed a novelty . . .

'Seven riders, including myself, journeyed to the (Maitland) showgrounds on a Sunday morning in October 1923 for a tryout. I was riding an old belt-driven Triumph and I rode it to capacity, but a rider named Bill Crampton came past me on a Norton so fast that he scared me off the track.

'Heads began to pop over fences . . . people on their way to church stopped and stared. One of my 42 committeemen hopped over the fence to see what all the racket was about and nearly fainted on the spot. That was the birth of dirt-track racing in the form we know it today.'

Johnnie again, in his book *Speedway Walkabout* published in 1977, after establishing that he had taken over as secretary of the West Maitland Hunter River Agricultural And Horticultural Society, recounted: 'Someone said: "There's money in this." "Bags of it," said the treasurer. They didn't fire me, they did worse, they let me organize a motorcycle race at a sports gathering which eventually took place on 15 December 1923.'

Note that date. A full year before A.J. Hunting's claim.

Hoskins, known as the 'shameless showman', was fond of putting the letters (*Liar.Hons*) after his name, and his enemies and rivals disparagingly referred to him as an Old Windbag, but those dates have been well documented in subsequent chronicles of the history of speedway racing.

There is also the claim by A.J. that 'I introduced dirt-track racing to England'. If that was the case, what was Jack Hill-Bailey and his Ilford Motorcycle And Light Car Club doing on Sunday 19 February 1928 behind the Kings Oak Hotel at High Beech?

What he was doing, according to his account on page 92 of *Roarin' Round The Speedways* was staging 'the first (official) speedway meeting ever held in England'. He wrote: 'As the person chiefly responsible for its organization I am telling, for the first time, what actually happened.'

In my 1995 publication, *A Fistfull Of Twistgrip*, which was carefully researched from contemporary records, Mr Hill-Bailey details the nightmare of 19 February 1928 when ten times the expected 3,000 spectators descended on the picturesque clearing in Epping Forest, Essex, to witness the extraordinary events of that amazing day.

Hill-Bailey disclosed: 'I remember very vividly how, in the midst of all our worries and troubles, Mr A.J. Hunting, the famous Australian promoter, found his way over to me and said: "My boy, you are doing it all wrong. This isn't the way to run a speedway meeting."

'I don't think I made any reply. How could I? I knew it was all wrong. Of course it was all wrong . . . (but) right or wrong, I said to the members of my committee: "We have started a ball rolling and goodness knows where it will stop." '

Yes, A.J. had arrived. And while it is true that he did bring over the early great Australian pioneer dirt-trackers some time before Hoskins arrived in Britain, and eventually set up International Speedways Ltd (ISL), which turned out to be the most powerful promoting company the sport has yet seen, he may well have been guilty of a Churchillian terminological inexactitude when he wrote his feature for *Answers*.

Tony Webb explains that A.J. was very experienced at promoting and financing speedway tracks by the time he arrived in England in 1928. He was a man to be listened to. His ISL speedway 'empire' went on to encompass White City, and Belle Vue Manchester, White City (London), Wimbledon, Harringay, West Ham, Stamford Bridge, High Beech, Crystal Palace, and Birmingham Hall Green.

And he launched *Speedway News*, a magazine dedicated to publicising those tracks, not all of which were actually owned by him. The magazine was edited for some years by Norman Pritchard who Hunting had brought from Australia with his original rider pioneers.

Historian the late Jim Shepherd in his *A History Of Australian Speedway* in 2004, explained: 'One myth that has been perpetuated over the years is that Hoskins and Hunting agreed to work together to bring Australian speedway to Great Britain. The pair were hardly on speaking terms.

'It was Hunting the investors really wanted. Hunting had leapfrogged Hoskins with his earlier departure from Australia and was firmly established by the time Hoskins arrived and determined to keep out all potential rivals.

'To be fair, Hoskins never attacked Hunting in print and it must be said that Hunting was an extremely tough businessman and a monopolist. This was evident in his refusal to allow any of his riders to ride at Wembley when Hoskins was the manager there in 1929 and desperate for top line riders.'

The star Australian experts, including Frank Arthur, Jack Bishop, Hilary Buchanan, Noel Johnson, Vic Huxley, Billy Lamont, Frank Pearce, Dicky Smythe, Charlie Spinks and Ben Unwin, plus Cecil Brown of the USA, were all contracted to Hunting's International Speedways Ltd. Only Lamont is reported to have defied ISL and ridden for Hoskins at Wembley because, said Lamont, Hoskins had given him his first rides in Australia.

Hunting was well ahead of Hoskins, 'The Shameless Showman', in recruiting high profile people to help promote the dirt-track sport.

The first meeting at Brisbane's Exhibition Showgrounds Speedway on 16 October 1926, was opened by the Hon William Lennon, Lieutenant General of Queensland. A.J. advertised the meeting as 'By Royal Patronage'.

At Davies Park, Brisbane, two of the many celebrities were aviator Charles Kingsford Smith, who made the first trans-Pacific flight from the United States to Australia, and explorer Sir Frank Hurley.

In England at first, Hunting was getting some negative Press. His answer was to get real royalty involved in lifting speedway's profile. King Alphonso of Spain and Princess Ingrid of Sweden were two of the first to accept an A.J. invitation.

Land and water speed record holders Sir Malcolm Campbell and Sir Henry Segrave, novelist Edgar Wallace and actresses Mae Bacon and Peggy O'Neil all followed as star guests.

Hunting was good at recruiting high profile celebrities to his speedways: Here author Edgar Wallace presents a trophy to Frank Arthur.

Yet, in little more than a year after arriving in England, Hunting left. Webb says: 'He did not tolerate fools lightly. He would have become increasingly frustrated with the way speedway was developing in England by the beginning of 1929, considering as an astute businessman that the bubble had burst after the initial honeymoon period. The ISL track at Hall Green, Birmingham had closed after seven meetings, and there were problems at London White City which would see its closure at the end of 1929.

'Therefore it was no surprise that he sought new pastures. Having spent the 1928-29 winter in South America on an exploration trip, he left London in July 1929 for South America, opening a track at La Huracane Speedway in Buenos Aires in the winter of 1929-30 and in 1930-31 he opened two more tracks.

'He was assisted in these ventures by his brother Frank, Belle Vue general manager H. L. Brookes and Brisbane-based Douglas motorcycle dealer Jack Harris.

'Hunting's doubts about the immediate future of speedway in England were confirmed when Stamford Bridge and Harringay closed in 1932 which left only Wimbledon as the remaining asset until 1937 when Ronnie Green took over.'

Archivist Ross Garrigan says: 'I have never found any concrete evidence as to just why Hunting quit International Speedways but he did like to be in control, he wanted to run things his own way. He did not like dealing with the Speedway Control Board, the Auto-Cycle Union and the Track Committee.'

It is thought that he was considered extravagantly generous with company funds by his directors and in early 1929 had a £15,000 handshake from ISL, which equates to close on half a million pounds in today's values. It is not known whether Hunting retained an interest in ISL after he left England.

A.J. Hunting's vision was always global.

According to Australian journalist Peter White in his book *100 Aussie Legends Of the Speedways*, when war came Hunting invented a unique thermos refrigeration system for the Australian army. There are 16 patents in his name in the national archives in Melbourne and Canberra.

Hunting retired from the business rat race to grow beet and return to toy making. He died in 1946 at his daughter's home in Melbourne while on a trip to a toy manufacturers' convention. He was 64.

Chapter 2
BUM'S THE WORD

THE most important part of a speedway rider's racing equipment, apart from his bike, of course, is . . . his crash helmet, which is designed to offer him the utmost protection in all circumstances and in any eventuality. After all, speedway is a hazardous business.

Seen here is a team of speedway riders putting their helmets to good use. You could say that their most precious piece of racing equipment is protecting . . . their most precious piece of racy equipment.

It is also apparent why the crash helmet is often referred to as a safety helmet.

This most remarkable illustration of a speedway scenario you have almost certainly never seen before was taken by that most celebrated photographer of track action Mr Michael Patrick (Speedway Snapper Retd. *See Page 73.)*

It is an example not only of a photo-journalist's ability to seize a moment of adversity and transform it into a unique and memorable achievement. It is also a tribute to Mike's unique powers of persuasion and also a remarkable comment on the complete trust in him shown by his young subjects.

Mike explained how it came about. He said: 'The shot was taken at Peterborough Press day on Tuesday, 21 March, 2000.

'Peterborough, the reigning League Champions, were let down by their team suit suppliers. Most of the team suits were not made in time for their Press day, so the Panthers were left shivering when it came to posing for the customary team photo.

'The shot itself was taken close to the team's dressing rooms away from the track and from prying eyes.'

So, who are these brave lads carrying out their public speedway obligations somewhat over and above the call of duty? From the left they are David Howe, Glenn Cunningham, Andre Compton, Ryan Sullivan, Stefan Andersson, Nigel Sadler and the man auditioning for a part in the Hairy Bikers television series, Sam Tesar.

As fine a body of men as you will find in any field of sporting endeavour, as I am sure you will agree. You could also say, of course, that they are displaying their . . . sponsors' logos to the best advantage.

Below left: Unique and memorable, but it's a bit of a bummer when your race suits don't turn up. Here the Peterborough team – and photographer Mike Patrick – turn their backs on adversity.

Below right: Keeping their sponsors happy – and preserving their modesty – the Panthers display a bold front.

Chapter 3
THE REG & WALLY SHOW

WHEN Reg Fearman and Wally Green got together to talk about speedway, it tended to be total mayhem. They rode the tracks as the cinders era was waning, but the sport at the time was full of swashbucklers, ruthlessly hard characters and established international stars highly jealous of their reputations.

I was privileged, on more than one occasion, to sit in on the *Reg And Wally Show* and listen to their stories – tall and otherwise – of their times and struggles as young hopefuls and team mates at West Ham, at a time that, apart from the early pioneering years, was one of the toughest in the history of the game in which to forge a career.

It's Showtime. A mature Wally (left) and Reg, the tellers of tall-ish tales, get serious.

Wally is now dead, but the pair of them delighted in recounting a multitude of lurid tales of the fights and feuds they were involved in, on and off the track. Wally was even in danger of being lynched at New Cross one night.

But he was a very modest aspiring speedway star who once called the Control Board and told them they were mad to pick him to ride for England.

Wally went on to captain England – but his grandchildren wouldn't believe him, until I produced a Test Match programme to prove it.

For instance there was speculation on whether there was a vendetta in the Ken LeBreton tragedy and whether their West Ham chum Cliff Watson knew the answer to everything…

The modern fan will probably want to know who exactly Reg and Wally are. Well . . .

REG FEARMAN: *Born London 1933. When he began his career with West Ham in 1949 he was the youngest contract rider in the game. Joined the Hammers after practice on the Custom House car park under the watchful eye of the great Australian Aub Lawson. Made his first appearance in competitive racing just after his 16th birthday in April 1949. He also rode for Stoke and Leicester. During his racing career he represented England in Tests against Australia, and went on to manage World Cup, World Pairs and international teams, chair the BSPA and, with Mike Parker, was instrumental in the resurrection of British speedway in the 1960s. He was President of the Veteran Speedway Riders Association in 1992.*

WALLY GREEN: *Born London 1922. Sank his wartime army gratuity into speedway equipment and, after being rejected by Arsenal Football club, Wembley and New Cross speedways, he was signed by West Ham in 1946. Loaned to Division Three Eastbourne in 1947, he helped them to win the first Third Division league championship and ended the season as their second best scorer behind Basil Harris. Moved to Hastings the following year where he coached many beginners and became Division Three Match Race Champion. Recalled to West Ham the next season, he was runner-up to Fred Williams at the 1950 Wembley World Final and went on to captain England, retiring in 1955. His other claim to fame is at the start of the war he was leading a convoy of 34 army lorries from Wandsworth bound for Bletchley and contrived to lose the lot by the time he got to what is now Brent Cross, for which he was banished to the Western Desert for the duration.*

So now you know. But I should warn you that some people may find parts of what they are about to read somewhat upsetting. Therefore if you are of a delicate disposition, look away now . . .

***

IT WAS, as they say, a jungle out there on the track – rough, tough and no place for the faint-hearted. Reg was very young, a mere schoolboy really. And Wally was an almost total innocent, who knew little or nothing about how to even put the right gear on a bike, nor did he seem to desire or have the inclination to match the raw aggression of the bigger and badder boys against whom he had to try and make a living and a name for himself.

In the end, they both became stars themselves. Reg was the youngest Test rider of his era. Wally, as we have seen, captained England and also missed becoming the 1950 World Champion to Fred Williams by one single, solitary point. Though which he would have considered the more personally satisfying I am not sure – I never thought to ask him.

Getting anywhere near the big time was a pitiless process. And in the school of speedway hard knocks the lessons came no more vivid, or stark, or chastening, than the

How it's done: schoolboy racer Reg – he hadn't got his licence yet – under instruction from West Ham star Cliff Watson.

events of Saturday, 1 July, 1950. Speedway, they discovered that night, is a deadly and dangerous game. It was the night 'Iron Man' Joe Abbott, veteran of innumerable crashes, broken bones and the pre-war Belle Vue team-of-all-the-talents, was killed at Bradford.

John Chaplin: *I turned up an old* Speedway Gazette *which carried a picture of Joe after the accident. He was up against the fence. The editor decided to run the picture and some rival magazines apparently hailed it as a scoop. But the editor of* Speedway News, *Sammy Samuel, didn't publish. He considered that to to do so would have 'overstepped the bounds of good taste and good journalism'. The* Gazette *Editor said that he appreciated 'the restraint exercised by those other contemporaries who did not publish the picture'. In my opinion he did what any proper journalist should do – publish and be damned.*

Reg Fearman: *Joe was dead on the track.*

JC: *Yes.*

RF: *That was the very first fatal accident I ever saw on the speedway.*

JC: *Did it look bad?*

On the way to stardom. Division Three Match Race Champion Wally (left) defends his title against Exeter's Bert Roger at Hastings. An interesting observation: There are no protective balls on the ends of their clutch levers. A later fatal accident resulted in their universal introduction.

Tragedy on the track: The crash that resulted in the death of veteran Iron Man Joe Abbott which so 'shook up' Wally and Reg, and some editors refused to print.

RF: *Well, no. Not really. They went into the corner and Joe slid off. I was hanging over the pit fence along with the other West Ham and Bradford riders, all having a look.*

JC: *According to the published records of that meeting, it was Heat 6, Joe's Odsal team partner was Eddie Rigg, and the opposition was West Ham's Lloyd Goffe and Eric Chitty. Joe fell in front of Lloyd Goffe who was too close to avoid hitting him. It was a bad day for speedway, Jock Shead of Halifax also died that day in a crash at Norwich.*

Wally Green: *If I never did anything else, I was probably the fastest gater that there ever was – probably through fear. I was absolutely terrific at getting out of the gate. Couldn't pass anybody. I was frightened of every bloody track. Except Wembley, funnily enough, I loved Wembley. I got to like West Ham, but Bradford was a nasty track. It was very similar to Hastings, although at Hastings the corners were a bit sharper.*

But what happened with Joe I don't know. I saw him lying on the ground with the ambulance people bending over him. And then one guy stood up and took his overcoat off and covered Joe with his overcoat, including his head. As they took him past us I noticed that his face was black – which wasn't too surprising because I think the track was cinders and he could have got a load of cinders in the face – but it was extra black.

And somebody said: "That doesn't look too good." I thought: "If you think about that, Wally, you won't want to ride." So I just dismissed it, put it completely out of my mind, and rode. When I came in after my last ride in the second half I said to someone: "How's Joe?" And he said:" How's Joe? Joe's dead" And I went to pieces. It absolutely shattered me. But the silly thing is I had known that, but had dismissed it.

RF: *We were all there. They said he was dead straight away. I was very young. It was the very first fatal accident I'd witnessed on the speedway and it shook us all up. Looking back, I'm surprised that the meeting carried on.*

WG: *The only other person I saw killed was Ernie Roccio. At West Ham in 1952. After we'd both retired, Jeff Lloyd and I were sitting talking somehwere – probaby in a pub – and we were talking about all the people who had been killed during our career. And it was 44. Close friends and people we'd raced against.*

RF: *They would all have been head injuries. They don't get that today. They all end up today in wheelchairs because our old pudding basin,* papier maché *helmets would give and then your head would hit the top of them, the webbing bands inside would break and you'd get a fractured skull. So many riders had fractured skulls in our day. I watched speedway from 1945 and was involved* *in promoting until 1985 and it was only in the last 10-15 years that people began to end up in wheelchairs. There were fewer fractured skulls, but with these full-faced helmets, the helmet holds the head steady but the shock goes down the spine.*

JC: *I once discussed this with Ivan Mauger because I'd noticed that in all his seriously competitive years he never rode in a full-faced helmet. I asked him why. He said that they were designed low at the back of the neck and people were getting hurt because of it and so he wouldn't wear one.*

RF: *He wore the space helmet – I've still got one – which comes down and protects the ears and the temple . . . I would never have worn a full-faced helmet. And look how many do end up in wheelchairs.*

JC: *I started going to speedway in 1946 when there were still deep cinder surfaces, and there would be horrendous crashes every night. But people used to just bounce up. And I thought it was because there was such a depth of surface that it maybe cushioned the falls.*

RF: *And our leathers were very heavy, with thick padding on the elbows and the shoulders and knees. Today they are like skins. And they go so much faster now. But of course today's tracks do have the air safety fences.*

JC: *And of course there is also unseen body armour.*

RF: *I was just thinking about Eddie Rigg, when he first came to West ham with Bradford. I mean, he flew round West Ham. He had the power on all the way. He was very aggressive.*

WG: *Well, he came, and we all walked to the fence. And somebody said: "Hey, come and look at this bloke, he's leading Lawson. Now not many people beat Aub Lawson round West Ham. It was Riggy and he was extending his lead. Anyway, he won the race. And somebody said: "Who is he?" Well, I was very friendly with Ron Clarke. He was captain of Bradford, but he lived in Mill Hill, half a dozen roads away from where my wife Hazel and I used to live. I went up to Clarkie and said: "Whos' this?" "Bloody hell," he said. "He's a bloody goer, he is."*

So, after the race, Riggy, got off his bike and he picked up this bottle – and he took a big swig. We used to have water in the pits, but this was yellow. And Cliff Watson, who was a nutcase (RF: He was a hypochondriac), said: "It's a drug. He must be on a drug!" Because he'd won his first three races and we were betting whether he would win his last race, against Malcolm Craven who was really going at the time.

And he did, he beat Craven. Riggy came in as usual, took a big slug out of this yellow bottle. Watson was walking around saying: "We've got to find out what's in there . . . we've got to find out what's in there." And I was going up to Clarkie and saying: "What's in that bloody bottle?" And he said: "Oh, that's a special potion." It turned out to be Lucozade. I don't know how we found out, but Lucozade had just come on the market and it was on sale up north but not down in the London area.

Now, Cliff Watson: if a guy started to do well, Cliff would walk up and measure with his feet the distance between the footrest and the centre of the back wheel. He'd come back and measure his own and then he'd measure mine. Then he'd say: "That's the answer, Greenie, we've got to move our footrest back one-and-a-half inches. And so everybody at West Ham moved their footrest an inch-and-half back.

RF: *On my engine plates I had two positions for the footrest. On the big tracks I'd bolt it in the rear position – about two inches to the rear – and then for small tracks, like New Cross and Harringay, I'd bolt it into the forward position so that your weight was further forward so that you could turn more easily – because our bikes were very difficult to turn.*

WG: *Could I suggest, Reg, that you are like seven foot tall – where did you put your legs?*

RF: *Never had any problem with my legs. But we were going to talk about Eddie Rigg . . . now Eddie Rigg was involved in the Ken LeBreton accident at the Sydney Sports Ground in 1951. I was there with Jack Parker's England team. Eddie Rigg and Ron Clarke were riding, and Eric Williams, it was the last race, Heat 18, of the second Test match. It was the last corner. Jack Parker and I had to stand on the centre green ready to walk across to the changing rooms after the race. Riggy was leading LeBreton and LeBreton went to fly round the outside of him, and Riggy moved over and LeBreton hit the fence and of course he died.*

JC: *In the sixty-odd years since the tragedy, there has been much discussion about the incident and whether or not there was a vendetta between the two men.*

Toughing it out: Reg challenging Harringay's Arthur Bush (outside) and Nobby Stock, with partner Fred 'Kid' Curtis behind.

Team mates at West Ham: Reg (far left), Frank Bettis, Kid Curtis, Wally, Aub Lawson, Malcolm Craven, Cliff Watson, Howdy Byford and George Wilks.

RF: *There had been a bit of grievance between them in the previous Test match. I think LeBreton had come under him and pushed him out at the Sydney Royale, and I remember Riggy saying: "I'll get him. I'll have him, I'll have him." I mean, he didn't mean to kill him. And that was it. There was one of the biggest funerals, and the courtege was miles long. I've never seen anything like it.*

WG: *I have never understood that aggressive side of some speedway riders. We knew who they were, and you sort of kept out of their way.*

JC: *Don't you think some aggression is necessary . . . ?*

WG: *Well, you've got to have a little bit of aggression . . .*

RF: *There's always an aggressive rider in each team. At least one. Most tracks at that time had a home dressing room and a visitors' dressing room. I can remember sitting in our dressing room with Aub Lawson, Eric Chitty, Malcolm Craven, Fred Curtis, Cliff Watson, Wally . . . and the trainer would come in and give us the programme for the night. The boys would look at the programme. They might say: "We've got New Cross tonight. Who's owed one? And someone would say: "The last New Cross meeting I rode in An Oldie stuffed me in the fence." And they'd say: "All right, we're out for An Oldie tonight, then."*

It was more likely to have been Cyril Roger . . . he was tough! But, I mean, I was 16 and I was out to get people like Fred Curtis's place as reserve. And when we met in the second half – well, they were out to get me. And that's how it was. It was very, very hard.

WG: *I had a few run-ins with Cyril Roger. He was a bloody marvellous rider. He was a good, very good, hard rider. We met in the Third Division when I was king of Hastings and he was king of Exeter, and he held the track record.*

Every Monday the first race of the night was an attempt on the record. I arrived there one Monday night and Hazel and I were on our honeymoon. Her family all came from Exeter. We'd booked into a hotel during the afternoon . . . now all I can tell you is that within 20 minutes of me leaving that hotel I broke the Exeter track record.

So when I came into the pits, Cyril grabbed his bike and said: "He's broken my track record. I'm not having that. I want to smash it."

Well, they told him: "No. Next Monday you can have a go." But he wouldn't have it and he started arguing with the marshals. So they shut the gates. Cyril picked up his bike, raised it right above his head, put it over the fence and laid it down on the track, jumped over, pushed himself off and went round to the starting gate. And he started shouting, so they said: "Oh, well, let him do it." But of course he didn't get it back, and he came up to me afterwards and he said: "Greenie, you bastard, don't ever try and take my record off me. He threatened me. He threatened me. That was the first brush we had.

Then he went up to New Cross, and some months later I went to West Ham. Well, I had to go and race at New Cross and I couldn't believe the size of this track. (New Cross's 'Frying Pan' track was 262 yards, the smallest in Britain at the time). No one had told me anything about gears, so I had the West Ham gear on. (The Custom House 440 yard quarter miler was the biggest in Britain then). You couldn't control the bike with the West Ham gear on round New Cross.

But, as I say, I was a brilliant starter. I took the lead on the first bend – how I managed to get round the first bend I'll never know. It was so small, so tight. I went like a bat out of hell. Got round that all right and went into the next bend. But I didn't know that Bert Roger (Cyril's brother) was trying to pass me on the outside.

It was my first time at New Cross, I had the wrong gear on and I was completely out of control. Hated the sight of the track. I thought I was going to hit the fence, but between me and the fence was Bert Roger. Well, Bert gets hooked up in the fence and the race is stopped. We come round to the pits and stop. They are dragging Bert out of the fence. Now Cyril Roger came out of the pits, grabbed me by the chest and lifted me off my bike with my legs dangling. He would have knocked me into the Old Kent Road, but fortunately for me, Aub Lawson grabbed his punching arm and stopped him.

To get into and out of New Cross you had to go under the grandstand. When I left that night, in my old banger with my bike on the back, as I got underneath the stand there was this sea of faces waiting for me. I thought it must have something to do with Bert Roger. They all descended on me, started bouncing the car, thumping the door, which I'd locked, tried to smash the windows, tried to pull my bike off the back. They were going to lynch me. But I managed to start inching forward and push them out of the way and I escaped.

That was a nasty experience, but there was another incident at West Ham. We were racing New Cross again. Cyril got the jump on me and I was lying second. As we went down the back straight, Cyril fell off. I tried to swerve, but . . . oops, too late . . . I ran right over him and broke his arm.

Cyril came up to me about a month later. He was still strapped up and he walked up to me and said: "You did that on purpose, didn't you?"

I said: "Don't be silly." And I hadn't. I was just too stupid to swerve. Of course I didn't do it on purpose. He said: "I'll get you, Greenie. If it's the last thing I do, I'll get you."

But from that day onwards, I never made the start if Cyril was in the race. I didn't want him behind me.

RF: *He was a very hard rider though. I remember being in front of him in one race at New Cross and as I came out of every corner I'd look round to see where he was. And there was Cyril Roger, and I could see his eyes were out like organ stops. You could see them through his gas goggles. And I thought if he gets close enough to me, he'll kill me.*

WG: *In all the years of racing, Cyril had run-ins with Jeff Lloyd and Aub Lawson. Neither of them were frightened of him. I was, I was terrified of Cyril Roger. Not Aub. He would take them all on.*

Below left: The chosen ones: Wally (centre) gets another England call-up at Wembley, with his West Ham team mates, Cliff Watson (left) and Jack Young, this time on the other side for Australia.

Below right: Putting on the style: Wally at West Ham hits the first bend ahead of Ray Moore (left) and Eric French of New Cross.

Wally does his bit for England at Belle Vue, even though he thought they were barmy to pick him. From the left standing: Arthur Forrest, Louis Lawson, Alec Jackson, Ken Sharples, Fred Williams. Sitting: Split Waterman, Bert Roger, Alan Hunt and Wally.

I still have all my England colours, you know. I told my grandchildren I've still got them, but they were all stuck together. I managed to separate them, and I now have them along one wall of my garage. I've got my first World Final race jacket, the No.4 when I was in the first race.

I've got the one when I was captain of England. But when they first chose me for England, I thought: this is ridiculous. The Test match was at Belle Vue, and when I found I was in the team I phoned up the Control Board. I told them I'd never scored more than five points at Belle Vue. It's barmy to put me in. They said: "We're not changing the team". And so I went up there the week before with West Ham. My mechanic kept saying: 'Well, you don't really try, do you?" I had to admit it was true. So he said: "Come on, why don't you just try, just for tonight?"

I was West Ham's highest point scorer. I scored 11 out of 12. The following week I went up there in the Test match. I was second highest scorer. Ken Sharples got 12, and Alan Hunt and I got 11 each, but we lost to Australia 58 - 50. And I never scored more than five points again in all the time I went there.

RF: In 1953, half way through the season, I went from West Ham to Leicester. It belonged to Allan Sanderson, who owned West Ham, Leicester and Coventry. I used to pick up Jock Grierson. He worked for Victor Martins doing their engines and stuff, and he also rode for Leicester. I used to pick him up at Palmers Green and away we'd go up to Leicester. He said this young lad Gerry Hussey, who was the son of family friends, wanted to ride on the speedway and Jock had made up a bike for him to go and practise at Rye House.

Gerry would come back to Jock and say: "This bike isn't very fast. I got it flat out and I'm not getting anywhere." Unknown to Gerry Jock had put in a restrictor so that he couldn't open it right out. Jock gradually reduced the restrictor and went along to Rye House to see him and he said he was amazed. We took him along to Leicester and he was phenomenal. He was a star overnight.

WG: And then they did a silly thing: they sent him to West Ham. West Ham was a marvellous team, especially for riders like me. They didn't really have any stars and you never had to fight for your position in the team. We didn't win many matches and when a good lad like Gerry Hussey came in you thought: Oh, blimey, I'll have to get my skates on.

I never considered Eric Chitty to be a star, nor Malcom Craven (see page 142). Aub was a star. But when you talk about Chitty, you're talking about the man who broke my collar bone – and he did it deliberately.

JC: *But he was your team captain . . .*

WG: *I had been loaned by West Ham to Hastings and I was called back to West Ham to be a reserve in an open meeting. In Heat 4 I had to go out with Chitty, and as I was a phenomenally fast starter I got out first and came out of the first turn in front. Chitty came alongside me on the outside and then cut onto the inside halfway down the straight. I came off and broke my collarbone.*

A couple of weeks later, still strapped up, I went along to West Ham to watch a meeting. Chitty kept walking past me all night in the pits – completely ignoring me. Towards the end of the meeting, he came up to me and stared me straight in the face and said to me: "I tell you something: don't ever try and beat me round West Ham." And he wagged his finger at me as if to say: I taught you a lesson.

The sequel to that came years later when I was second highest point scorer and we drew Edinburgh in some cup competition at Edinburgh. Of course the king of Edinburgh was Jack Young. I won my first race and in my second race I had Eric Chitty with me as my partner – who was reserve then – against Jack Young. I was concentrating on trying to beat Jack Young, which was almost impossible because virtually nobody beat Jack Young round Edinburgh.

Terrifying: hard man Cyril Roger on the rampage at New Cross for England.

It doesn't get much better . . . Wally gets his hand on the World Championship trophy at the 1950 Wembley Final. He was runner-up to Fred Williams (centre) and Graham Warren was third.

Chitty came up to me and said: "Will you help me round the first corner?" I more or less agreed I would – though I knew I wouldn't after what he did to me. The tapes went up and I shot out with Youngie behind me and we went down the back straight. Three quarters of the way round the next bend Youngie came past me like a dose of salts – he came past me so fast . . . and just then the red lights came on.

Chitty had fallen off. And he never raced again. I think he'd fractured his skull. And I thought that perhaps if I'd helped him round the first corner maybe he wouldn't have been hurt. And then I thought: You can't say that Wally, he didn't consider you when he broke your collarbone, and he did it deliberately.

I met Chitty once in Toronto. He was with Malcolm Craven who was working at the local airport as an air traffic controller. Now that was a laugh . . . because Craven was always pie-eyed.

There was a fight in the Belle Vue pits one night between Cyril Brine and Malcolm's mechanic. Cyril came up to me and said: "Craven's pissed." I knew he was because he'd travelled up with me. Malcolm took over from Fred Curtis in knowing the opening and closing times of every pub from London to every speedway track.

This night, at the last pub we'd called into on the way to Belle Vue, he had an empty gin bottle with him. He ordered a tonic water, for me, and six gin and tonics which they poured into his empty bottle ready for when we left the meeting.

Anyway Briney said he was going to report Malcolm to the authorities and Malcolm's mechanic sort of took Briney on. But Cyril wasn't too sure about having a fight. He didn't want to get too involved so he didn't report him.

I used to travel with a length of rope in the back of the car, because when Malcolm finished these six gin and tonics, he'd put the empty bottle down, go to sleep and eventually he would fall on me. Now if someone is drunk and falls on you, you can't drive properly. They are so heavy. I used to stop, get the rope out, lower the front and back windows pass the rope through, round Craven and tie him to the side of the car.

RF: But he had this beautiful 1938 Buick Straight-Eight. It was immaculate. Every Tuesday night at West Ham, he'd drive it in through the big double gates at the stadium, walk across the concourse and straight into the bar. He'd order two large gin and tonics, then go down to the dressing rooms and get changed. Then go out and get a maximum.

WG: But when you talk about stars. Split Waterman (see page 95). Now he was a star. Not that he was as good as Jack Young – or anywhere near – but the world loved him. Wherever I've *travelled in the world everyone asks if I know Split Waterman. They don't ask: do you know Aub Lawson or Jack Parker or Fred Williams . . . but do you know Split?*

THERE is a postscript to all this. Soon after I had given him the Test Match programme to show his grandchildren that he had indeed captained England, I received a letter from Wal. It read:

I would like to thank you personally for giving me the 1954 programme of the Test Match against Australasia at West Ham when I was captain of England.

My partner that day was Freddie Williams, the fantastic Wizard of Balance Peter Craven was only second reserve and we raced against Jack Young, Aub Lawson and Barry Briggs. Great days. Fantastic memories

I was interested to note that in the programme Freddie Williams scored only five points and I as captain scored only six. The great Split Waterman scored only seven, so between us we scored only 18 points. Fortunately for England Arthur Forrest scored 15 points and Brian Crutcher was top scorer of the night with 17 points.

Thanks to Brian and Arthur I am able to tell my grandchildren I was captain of England on the night we beat Australasia 60 points to 48.

Thanks for the memory, John.

> *WALLY GREEN*
> *(World No.2 1950)*
> *Arkley, Hertfordshire*

WHAT Wally was far too modest to mention was that the match report said: 'Skipper Green opened magnificently with a tearaway win over his opposite number Jack Young.'

Wal shows his back wheel to a couple of multi-World Champions – Jack Young on the left and Barry Briggs.

Chapter 4
AKKO'S EPIC NIGHT

THIS little speedway drama is based on a true story. Well, actually it *IS* a true story, and as with all the best dramas it is a tale of adversity and eventual triumph.

There are precious few fields of sporting endeavour left in this cynical, win-at-any-cost, modern world where the contestants can actually elevate the human condition. But in this particular instance, speedway is definitely one of them.

The shining example of such an event is *Akko's Epic Night.* As well as disaster and triumph, those well-known imposters – as Rudyard Kipling described them in his famous poem *If* – there is the requisite touch of pathos, to tug at the heartstrings. But, above all, it is simple.

Trust me, it is a story that has everything, though in equally cynical media sound bite terms it can be dismissed in a mere two paragraphs. Thus:

'The brilliant comeback of Arthur Atkinson overshadowed everything else in West Ham's first round meeting of the World Championship. The West Ham ace had been out of the saddle for nearly a month with a broken collarbone, and he returned for this meeting to sweep the deck.

'It was the real Akko. Riding with his head and grim determination, there was no one to touch him. His shoulder strapped up and every effort a torture, he won all of his five races to secure 15 points and prove he is definitely in the running for Bluey Wilkinson's crown.'

To discover, behind that matter of fact report, the real drama in terms of human courage and speedway achievement, you will have to come with me across three-quarters of a century to a distant 1939 July night in the Custom House pits in East London. It was a night with 'Epic' stamped clear all the way through it, a night for wise old men to recall, and young men, poised for equally epic accomplishments, to draw inspiration from.

There were 30,000 witnesses to greatness that night. The terraces were packed with eager fans to see the drama unfold.

Close encounter. Leading the pack in his familiar trademark white scarf and dimpled leathers, Arthur Atkinson ahead of a couple of real veterans, Colin Watson on the outside and Charlie Spinks.

Almost a month previously the Hammers' Yorkshire-born idol Arthur 'Akko' Atkinson had taken a tumble at the track he considered his jinx circuit, Wimbledon, while competing for the famous Laurels. The fall had fractured a collarbone. It was a serious setback for Akko who had been in brilliant form that summer. He had become the darling of the Dockland crowds in succession to their dynamic little hero Bluey Wilkinson.

Bluey, who had thrilled the fans for so long, was the reigning World Champion. He had won the crown at Wembley the previous season and then, at the very pinnacle of his popularity and fame, had quit to become the promoter at Sheffield.

Nothing that his devastated West Ham boss Johnnie Hoskins could do was able to change the little Australian's mind. He stayed retired from active racing, and it allowed Atkinson, whose brilliance had been somewhat overshadowed by Wilkinson, to come into his own.

On that July evening the stricken Atkinson appeared in the West Ham pits, injured, pale and suffering, with his damaged shoulder heavily strapped. He was riding in defiance of his doctor's orders because he knew he must take part in the meeting to stand any chance of qualifying for that year's World Final.

Not only that, but he knew he had to score heavily because of a bonus points system which riders carried with them to the big night. It had cost Wilkinson the Championship in 1936 when he had ridden unbeaten in the Final only to be denied the title because he hadn't taken enough bonus points with him.

When Atkinson went out onto the track for his first ride, his face was a pale as the pure white scarf he always wore round his chin. It was an all-West Ham race. He was up against his team mates, but there were no favours being done . . .

The darlings of Docklands. Arthur (on the bike) and Bluey Wilkinson receive the trophy for winning the national Best Pairs title at Harringay in 1937.

Tommy Croombs, the white line king, flashed into the lead from the tapes with Eric Chitty second, Akko third and Harold 'Tiger' Stevenson last. There was no change for three laps, then came a frenzied scream from the terraces. A blue-helmeted figure surged past Chitty and overtook Croombs. The sick man had been holding back, conserving his strength until the chequered flag was in sight. On the final bend the race was his.

A weary but happy Akko rode with head bowed into the pits to sink down on an out-of-the-way bench away from the crowds. He did not want to talk, merely to concentrate on holding the pain in his shoulder at bay until his next ride. There were four more to go – sixteen agony-filled laps.

Heat five, and a new hushed expectancy settled over the crowd. Activity in the pits grew still as the slight figure of Atkinson stepped forward bravely for his second ride of the night.

This time there as no waiting. He gated like a dream. Wembley's Tommy Price – a future World Champion – chased him vainly. His West Ham team mate Jimmy Gibb came in a battling third. Billy Dallison of Southampton, badly away, fell on lap two. Akko, inspired, led all the way and tacked another valuable three points onto his score.

Back on his solitary bench in the pits Akko managed to weakly acknowledge his admirers in the crowd. Then he closed his eyes as the waves of pain overwhelmed him once more.

Yet Atkinson's was not the only drama of the night. Charlie Spinks took a spectacular last bend tumble in front of his home crowd in Heat six. Ron Johnson of New Cross crashed while leading Middlesbrough's George Greenwood in the next race.

Then it was Heat nine, Atkinson's third ride.

It seemed that the fairy tale must end. Johnson, none the worse for his previous fall, streaked from the tapes ahead of Spinks and another Hammer, Dick Geary. Atkinson appeared to have no fight left in him. It seemed that at last nature's searing pain was about to become just too much for his remarkable courage and gallantry.

But, defiantly, he moved up one, passing Geary, and there was a roar from the crowd as he closed on Spinks. But with less than one lap left Johnson still held on to his commanding lead. Hoskins, who had seen speedway's cruel retribution so many times over the years, leaned in sorrow over the pit rails convinced he was about to watch his rider succumb to the inevitable.

Then a great roar rippled round the vast stadium. Eric Chitty sent the Hoskins hat flying, an excited and nervous reporter dropped a glowing cigarette between his jacket and shirt. They had seen Atkinson catch Johnson on the final bend and at the flag another three almost unbelievable points went onto the Akko score.

He was by then so weak he could hardly raise a smile as he was congratulated. He had to be assisted from his machine back in the pits. Almost as soon as he was cleaned up from the last effort he had to be on his feet again for his fourth ride, this time in a really tough line-up which included Belle Vue's Eric Langton, the former World No.2, and Harringay's Norman Parker *(see page 40).*

Perhaps adrenaline, still flowing after the win over Johnson, had dulled the excruciating pain in his shoulder and enabled Akko to win easily.

The meeting, and the drama, now centred entirely on Atkinson. The partisan home crowd sensed the theatricality of what was unfolding before them. There was one more ride for Atkinson, which he needed to win to end the night on a maximum. The tension in the air could be almost grasped as the riders went to the tapes for Heat seventeen.

Only Atkinson would ever know what superhuman effort it took to gather his remaining strength for that final ride. To the crowded terraces where the fans stood in mesmerized expectation, and to the hushed pits where racing colleagues watched in admiration, the hunched figure seemed totally alert.

It could have been that Akko was 'on automatic', employing the speedway racer's sixth sense which seems to come into play on such occasions. When the tapes flashed up he was away . . . leaving Belle Vue's Bob Harrison and George Greenwood trailing. Wembley's George Wilks suffered an engine failure before reaching the first bend.

Atkinson's last ride had 'maximum' written all over it. He led all the way, winning as he pleased. When it was all over he rode straight through the pits. The staggering performance of the man earned the unashamed admiration of his fellow riders, but his shouted farewell was swept away on the tide of emotion the night had produced. Even the hard-headed Hoskins was visibly carried away.

An even closer encounter: Arthur, during his brief comeback after the war with Harringay, powers under Bristol's Eric Salmon with team mate Nobby Stock just behind.

Atkinson's return to world class form was almost immediate after that momentous night. He qualified for the World Final and was England's main hope for speedway's supreme prize against the powerful challenge of that season's World Championship favourite, America's Cordy Milne *(see page 80)*.

The pity of it all was . . . that Atkinson's brave defiance of the very gods of speedway was in vain. We shall never know whether Akko would have won the World title for the first time for England. Five days before the Final was due to be staged at Wembley England declared war on Hitler's Germany.

In the words of a chronicler of the day, 'speedway racing became nothing more than a wonderful memory'.

Just like Atkinson's Epic Night.

Trading his leathers for a promoter's suit with his Hammers in 1948. From left, co-promoter Stan Greatrex, Aub Lawson, Cliff Watson, Eric Chitty on the bike, Howdy Byford, Arthur, Kid Curtis, Malcolm Craven and Tommy Croombs.

Chapter 5
THE INCREDIBLE PARKERS

JACK – THE GREAT PRETENDER

THERE are people who insist that Jack Parker was the greatest speedway rider never to have won a World Championship. One of them was Jack Parker.

Once, I was naïve enough to ask him who he considered the greatest speedway rider in the sport's history. There was a moment's pause, during which others who, like me, had been hanging on the great man's every word, waited breathless for his response.

Jack laid his hand across his chest and, in his unblemished Birmingham accent, said: 'Well, modesty forbids . . . ' Then, in almost the same breath, he said: 'No. Eric Langton. Eric was totally brilliant. Eric had everything.'

There is no doubt that Jack Parker considered himself a man apart when it came to the speedway game. And it is true. He was. His sustained record of excellence over a racing career that spanned twenty-six years is proof that he was the possessor of a unique talent.

His answer to my question, though apparently swaggeringly arrogant to anyone unaware of the man's achievements, was not as the dictionary defines arrogance – 'an

Classic action from two maestros of the cinders art that filled Wembley with weekly FA Cup Final-sized crowds during the early post-war boom seasons, Jack Parker leads rival captain Bill Kitchen at the Empire Stadium in 1946.

Above left: *The greatest. Test match tactical talk between Eric Langton (left), the man who was totally brilliant and had everything, according to Jack (right).*

Above right: *Parker's finest hour … champion at last: Jack hoists the trophy after winning the world title substitute, the British Speedway Riders Championship, at Wembley in 1947.*

exaggerated opinion of one's importance'. Neither was it conceit, which can be offensive.

It was more the mark of the supreme egotist. It was the natural expression of absolute confidence in his own ability. It is a quality that breeds winners: ask multi speedway World Champions Ivan Mauger and Tony Rickardsson, ask cyclist Bradley Wiggins, ask F1's Michael Schumacher, ask football's Pele, ask cyclist Victoria Pendleton, ask rowing's Sir Steve Redgrave, ask tennis star Roger Federer . . . or any other true sporting great.

Even now, sixty years after the curtain came down on Parker's racing career, anyone who knows anything about speedway history considers that Jack was the best never to have worn the world crown.

And though acknowledged as the finest English exponent of the cinders art, Parker once confessed: 'I was never a true professional. I was never in it for the trophies.'

Yet, according to his brother Norman, the brilliant early post-war Wimbledon captain, in the deep, dark recesses of Jack's private mind, the world title was what he coveted most of all. He would never admit it publicly, but it was to his eternal regret that the nearest he came to winning the supreme prize was runner-up to Tommy Price in 1949.

So if, like me, you were ever booby-trapped into trying to discuss with him who was the best speedway rider never to have won the World Championship, you had only yourself to blame if you ended up shell-shocked.

Check out the names: Vic Huxley, Jack Biggs, Split Waterman, Vic Duggan, Max Grosskreutz, Graham Warren, Dennis Sigalos, Eric Langton, Wilbur Lamoreaux, Cordy Milne, Arthur Atkinson, Brian Crutcher, Aub Lawson, Sverre Harrfeldt, Zenon Plech, Les Collins, Leigh Adams . . . . need I go on? I'm sure you have your own very worthy candidates.

And Norman, with whom Jack formed an international partnership for England that has never been surpassed, confessed to me that he would have laid down his own life had it meant his brother being crowned king of the speedway world.

Jack, of course, always claimed he WAS World Champion – four times actually – or the equivalent anyway, and cited his British Championship of 1931, a 'world championship' in Paris the same year *(which I have been unable to verify . . . JC)*, the Star Championship won at Wembley in 1934 and the Speedway Riders Championship – a World Championship substitute – at Wembley in 1947.

One of Parker's most fierce rivals always likened him to the comedian who was unable to rest until he had played Shakespeare's Hamlet. But if Jack could never quite win the right to wear the King Of Speedway mantle he had 'royal' status thrust upon him by my old mentor Basil Storey *(see page 108)*, the influential Editor of *Speedway Gazette*.

In the edition for 9 August 1947 in the feature *Will Shakespeare's Piece* there appeared the headline: *Hamlet, Prince Of Cinders (Or As You Like it)*. It referred to 'Parker the great' as 'prince of the world of leather clad heroes', and the peg the report was hung on was the fact that Parker had amassed a mere five points in his first Speedway Riders Championship qualifier. His lowly score was put down to the fact that 'England's most brilliant maestro is inclined to be slap-happy – a superb tactician but no technician. He persists in tinkering about with motors.'

But, went on the narrative, 'Parker is such an overwhelming personality, so great an exponent of the cinders art that one is inclined to forget the machine in the all-embracing admiration of the man.

'So magnificent is the Parker legend that it is possible to believe that Jack, called upon to ride for the kingdom, is capable of grabbing any old iron that chances to be lying around and hurtling his way to triumph. I am almost tempted to believe that of Parker myself.

'What can you make of a maestro who goes forth to ride in an important qualifying round of the Speedway Riders Championship and, besides other misadventures, loses his clutch in the middle of a race? It is like Sir Thomas Beecham stepping onto the rostrum, to conduct the William Tell Overture, minus his trousers.

'But there is not a fan in speedway who dares to think that Jack is not capable of scoring at least 35 points in his three remaining meetings to assure himself a place in the Wembley final. In fact, if Jack Parker doesn't qualify they might as well postpone the final until he does so.'

Such was the magic of the man. In fact, in his three remaining qualifiers Parker scored 36 points and went on to win the final. But, of course, it wasn't an official World Championship.

Jack was ordered to attend his first speedway meeting by his bosses at the BSA motorcycle company where he was a works tuner and competitions rider. He had heard of the new sport from Lionel Wills, the English traveller who had chanced upon the broadsiding spectacular in Australia.

At Whitsun 1928, at the age of twenty-three, Jack turned up reluctantly at High Beech in Epping Forest to give this dirt-track racing the once-over. He was not best pleased because if had meant cancelling a weekend break on the coast. He didn't know it, but he was about to meet his destiny.

At High Beech he was greeted by a man in a wide brimmed hat, Jack Hill-Bailey, who was running the show. He invited Jack to strip down his road machine and try speedway for himself.

Jack recalled: 'I didn't know how to broadside, and I didn't use my head enough. I won my first outing by too big a margin and next time out they set me back on the scratch line.'

He did well enough to be invited to ride at Wimbledon against the top Australian expert Vic Huxley, and though he would have preferred to sample the delights of London's West End, the prize money – £20 win or lose – was an offer he couldn't refuse. His weekly pay at BSA was £3.15shillings at the time.

Parker was among the first English riders to seriously challenge the might of the early Australian pioneers and, with the introduction of organised team racing in 1929 he soared to the very top, captaining every side he rode for: Coventry, Southampton, Clapton and Harringay before the war, and Belle Vue after the war.

Parker always had an astute business sense and drove a hard bargain, not only for the

The perfect pair. The Parker brothers' almost telepathic international on-track understanding had no equal. Opening for England was their speciality, here being demonstrated in a Test match at Belle Vue with Norman on the outside and Jack on the inside.

Jack adored the ladies, and they certainly loved him, judging by the effect his charismatic personality is having on these female fans. The celebrity stars of today never had it so good.

men he represented in later years as chairman of the Speedway Riders Association (SRA) – the riders' union – but himself as well. His signing on fee when he joined Southampton was disguised as a payment for painting the stands.

With the expansion of speedway into a serious worldwide sporting spectacle, Parker became one of the elite performers of the tracks. He rode in the historic first official Test match against Australia at Wimbledon in 1930 and thereafter was rarely out of the international arena. He reached all the pre-war World Finals and there were the occasional individual successes too – the most outstanding of these was taking the British Championship from Huxley in a classic confrontation at Plough Lane.

He rode in the Belle Vue wartime meetings, but without a great deal of distinction. Wilf Plant, who rode against Parker during that time, recalled that Jack was on a straight £40 a meeting and he, who didn't enjoy star status, was paid £10.

He said: 'Jack seemed to get paid for doing nowt. But he had the name of course, he was a brilliant rider.

'I once said to him: "Jack, I'm honoured to have beaten you here at Belle Vue tonight." And he said: "Well, I'm in speedway for the money. I'm not riding my guts out. I can beat you any time I like, and I could beat anybody here." '

When team strengths were pooled after the war in 1946, Parker was allocated to Belle Vue, and with the renewed serious competition, the Parker brilliance returned. In that year's Championship final at Wembley he had four winning rides, but a broken steel shoe strap caused him to fall in his second, the vital encounter with eventual champion Tommy Price.

As leader of the Aces, he helped bring the glory days back to the north, inspiring the side to three wins in the National Trophy and, frustratingly, five times as league runners-up to Wembley in the first six post-war seasons.

Then, as age began to catch up with the old maestro, his brilliance and that of Belle Vue started to fade.

Why did the major prize continue to elude Parker? Double World Champion Fred Williams, who literally emerged from his novice chrysalis into virtually fully-formed star status during one of the Parker-led England winter tours of Australia, insists it was Jack's well-known disposition to be slap-happy about his equipment.

Fred said: 'We would all arrive for a World Final with immaculate bikes. We'd look at Parker's and it would be filthy and there would be rollers missing from his chains. His machines would be a shambles. I don't know how he rode them.'

To many, Parker's finest hour was the 1947 Speedway Riders Championship final at Wembley when he and Norman outrode Australia's Vic Duggan, whose incredible form

The Master: Jack wears The British Match Race Championship Golden Helmet and cradles the magnificent accompanying trophy, the Warwick Vase, after yet another successful defence of the title he held for so long it became known as Parker's Pension.

that year had made him a cast-iron certainty to win. When Jack swept past Duggan to virtually clinch the title in a momentous Heat 8, even hard-bitten and cynical reporters in the Press seats leaped to their feet cheering in admiration.

Parker's real mastery showed itself in the British Match Race Championship Golden Helmet series between 1946 and 1951. It had begun in 1931, and he took part in 26 contests overall, winning 22, losing three and having to retire once through injury. During one period he defeated 13 consecutive challengers. Harringay's Vic Duggan and West Ham's Aub Lawson took the helmet from him temporarily. He always got it back, losing it finally to Harringay's Split Waterman in 1951.

Parker's achievement was much to the chagrin of Ove Fundin, of Norwich and Sweden, who won the World Championship five times. Like Williams before him, Fundin emerged during another Parker-led winter tour of Australia in 1954-55, and, before retiring, badly wanted to do better than Parker in match racing.

But though Fundin also took part in 26 contests, he won 19 and lost 6 with one challenge not raced. So, even though he won five world titles and Parker didn't win one, he was unable to equal what Parker had done in the Golden Helmet match races.

The post war series was sponsored initially by the *Sunday Pictorial* newspaper and it carried a bounty for the title holder of £1 a day. Jack held it for so long that it became known as Parker's Pension.

He employed a highly personalised brand of psychological gamesmanship. He also perpetrated the myth that he could casually grab any clapped out old bike and win on it.

The reality was that he had team mates' machines meticulously prepared. He would theatrically discard his own and have one of theirs wheeled out – a move that invariably fazed his opponent.

On one famous occasion at Birmingham he completely psyched out his challenger, Eric French of New Cross, by pretending to fall asleep astride his machine during the pre-match preliminaries.

The Parker philosophy was this: 'If you spend hours polishing the bike so that it shines like new it has the effect of making your opponent think you have a supercharged machine and that to beat you he will have to go like the clappers. But if your machinery is, shall we say, looking a bit on the uncared for side, he'll get the idea that he won't have to try too hard. It's a simple psychological trick but it's a fact of life.

'The bike I had for the Golden Helmet affairs was clean and polished. It was made to look special. The unnoticed bike I left leaning against the fence had been given a spot of extra treatment.

'No, it wasn't oversized, it conformed to all the rules.

'I'm not being big-headed, but I always had a strong belief in my technical riding ability. I was good enough to beat anyone in a one-to-one encounter, but it helps if you have some kind of advantage.

'I'd ride out of the pits on my spit-and-polish bike, revving it – showing off if you like – but at the gate I'd turn back and return to the pits. My opponent would invariably follow me back to the pits rather than stay revving at the gate. Making sure he could see what I was doing I'd fling my bike down and grab the spare one from against the fence, pick up a spanner and pretend to make some minor adjustment, then set off for the start again.

'The con was completed when, half way there, the bike would stop. I'd have the pushers-off get me going again and by then my opponent usually thought it was the end of the line for JP. But it was truly amazing how that old JAP would respond. Yes, it's true, there were bits of string and wire to be seen, apparently holding it together, but I assure you they had no real purpose, except to kid my opponent.'

This way he had of being in control by wickedly stage-managing events, tactics designed primarily to create anxiety in his opponents, he once pulled on me. At a special *Speedway Star* magazine fan-festival weekend I had arranged to present an all-star question and answer session. A full house was eager to hear from a line-up that included World

Champions Tommy Price and Fred Williams, Birmingham captain Phil 'Tiger' Hart *(see page 132)* and Jack. When the four of us – Tommy, Fred, the Tiger and me – took our places on the stage there was no sign of Parker. I introduced them all to the audience . . . and there was still no sign of Parker.

I could see his shadowy figure moving about in the gloom offstage and I could feel myself getting anxious until, when he considered the moment was right, he made a grand entrance, timed to perfection. He wanted to create the impression that he was *The Star*, you see. And of course he *was*.

I commend to you a eulogy to Parker by the late Coventry boss Charles Ochiltree, who should have known because he was very closely associated with Jack, the prime mover behind the reopening of Brandon after the war.

In *Stenner's Speedway Annual* for 1949, with the title *Jack Parker, Thinker, Dreamer, Man Of Action*, Ochiltree observed that JP was capable of serving up more dazzling performances than ever, usually when least expected. Ochiltree wrote: 'Jack still fools them all – even those who have watched him through the halcyon days of an absorbing career.

'Losing the silliest of races and causing critics to shake their heads, he will suddenly rocket to new heights, demand fresh recognition and earn even greater esteem by defeating the headline-making youngsters and smashing with seemingly effortless ease decades-old track records.'

It should be remembered that, at the time, Parker was well into his forties. It couldn't happen today.

In the 1970s, long after he had retired from the track, I interviewed him. What he said about speedway racing was extraordinarily prophetic.

He said: 'Since I stopped racing they have made the tracks easier to ride. What they are doing is making them faster and fewer mistakes are made. I saw some racing from Belle Vue *(the old Hyde Road)* and it seems the track is getting to be a circle. If they finish up racing round a ring you won't get overtaking.

'Everything seems to be made for faster racing. But what's the difference? The public don't want to see us going two or three miles an hour faster – and anyway a National bus on the M1 would leave us for dead. They go much faster than we do.

'And what is everybody doing paying thousands of pounds for a speedway bike when wonderful machines can be made for a fifth of the price and put on a marvellous show?

The natural leader. Captaining England in Australia. The troops, from the left, are Howdy Byford, Fred Williams, Dent Oliver, Jack, Oliver Hart, Cyril Roger, Ron Clarke and Jack's nephew Dennis Parker.

The new World Champion, Tommy Price – England's first official title holder in 1949 – takes the winner's place on the Wembley victory lap of honour. And Jack has to take a back seat with Louis Lawson.

It was to Jack's eternal regret that he was denied the title he coveted most of all, the World Championship, and has to watch Tommy Price take the top prize in the first post-war World Final at Wembley in 1949. Third was Louis Lawson, so at least England could claim the top three.

In my opinion there should be 20 bikes at every track, all numbered, and they should be drawn for. They would all have to be kept in good order because the home captain could get any one. We would all have the same bikes then, and you'd soon know who was the best. It would have suited me because I could ride any bloody thing.'

Jack adored the fans and used them to read a race, especially during the Golden Helmet challenges which attracted huge crowds and massive publicity, in spite of being derided by commentators as a throwback to the early undignified circus side-show days of the sport.

He said: 'The crowds were wonderful. They used to push me down the straights. The pleasure of knowing they are with you is incredible. In the Match Races they would hang over the fence and I could tell by their behaviour how far away the man behind me was because I used to say that I never looked back. I always said that a man who looks back doesn't know his business.

'When I was behind it never used to worry me because I could recite to you the errors in style that every rider had, and I knew just where and how I could pick them off. It was very simple if you knew the business.'

Reflecting . . . on what might have been: Jack lost in his own thoughts caught at a quiet moment in the pits.

And the dangers of speedway racing? He had considered those too. He said: 'You cannot imagine anyone being viciously foul as competitors are in other sports. It just doesn't belong in speedway. It is dangerous, and some riders are wilder than others, but if anyone was deliberately ferocious they wouldn't last long.

'There *is* the possibility of getting hurt, there is no doubt about that. But you accept it. And a certain amount of danger is acceptable. In fact it's quite nice.'

Jack adored the ladies too. He had organized and led England tours to Australia since the 1930s, and he invited the emerging Ove Fundin with fellow Swedes Ulf Ericsson and Goran Norlen on what proved to be his final trip for the 1954-55 winter season. On the voyage the three Swedes were sharing a cabin and Ove Fundin told me of this escapade.

He said: 'Jack was a bit of a ladies' man. He tried everything. One night we were all trying to get some sleep when we heard Jack come into the cabin with someone, and we heard a girl's voice say: "Jack, are you sure those Swedish boys are asleep? And Jack said: "Yes, yes, yes, of course. Just be quiet and come on in."

'And then they got going. Having their bit of fun. After a while Ulf Ericsson said – not shouted, but he wasn't quite whispering: "Are you going to be finished soon, Jack, so we can all get some sleep?"

'Well, everything went quiet for a few seconds, and then we heard Jack and the girl leave the cabin.'

Ove also remembered being approached by Jack at one of the old Veteran Dirt Track Riders Association's annual dinners. Ove said: 'Jack came up to me and showed me a letter from a girl. He said: "You must read this." I can't remember exactly what it said, but it was something like: "It's amazing, a man of your age *(Jack was then in his late seventies)* being able to satisfy a young girl like me the way you did. And it's not like any of the young men I go out with who are finished within minutes – and there you are who can go on almost for hours"'.

It was looking back – the thing he said he never did – that cost Jack his brilliant career. But he was not on a speedway machine. He was testing a midget racing car at the Sydney Sports Ground speedway. Jack's luck ran out in February 1953 . . . on Friday the 13th . . .

After the crash: Jack displays the results of being careless by looking round during a midget car test in Australia. He has a prominent black eye and his arm is heavily bandaged because it was badly scalded in the accident. The fabulous career was virtually over.

Back on a bike at seventy-one for speedway's 50th anniversary at Hackney. In a special match race – what else? – Jack celebrates the occasion by beating contemporary England captain Malcolm Simmons who was quietly advised: 'Would you mind letting Jack win? It would be really good for everyone if he did.'

when he took a quick glance behind.

In the fraction of a second that took, the car hit the fence and rolled. Jack's skull was fractured, a shoulder was injured and he suffered scalds from the exploding radiator. For a while he was on the hospital danger list.

'I was careless,' he said later.

Jack did ride again, but he was never the world class force he had been. His final racing season in England was 1954. By then he and his diminishing band of original pioneers had been elbowed aside by the young newcomers: Peter Craven was the new star at Belle Vue, there was Alan Hunt at Birmingham, Eddie Rigg at Bradford, Brian Crutcher at Wembley, Jack Young at West Ham and Geoff Mardon at Wimbledon. The high scoring Parker talent was reduced to a mere 64 points in his final year for the Aces.

But he even had an answer for that. He said: 'I never slowed up because of that accident. My accountant told me to have a poor year for tax purposes.'

More Parker kidology . . . or what?

Jack rode for England, invariably as captain, on 96 occasions. Maybe with unofficial internationals he made it 100-plus, but the record books come up with only 96. That figure is the more meritorious because in those days there were no World Cups and no World Pairs championships. There was only one five-match series of Tests in England and they took place once a month during the season. There were also the series he organised as rider-manager in Australia – not all official.

What the old rascal never confessed to me was that on one memorable occasion, Jack Parker, the England captain, actually rode for Australia. It was an England v Australia 'international' at Odsal on Saturday, 1 September 1945, billed as the twelfth meeting.

Maybe he didn't mention it because he scored only three points in four rides – but, as in the wartime meetings, perhaps he wasn't really trying.

Mind you, it was a bit of a polyglot 'Australian' side. It included three other Englishmen, Tiger Hart, Syd Littlewood and Ron Clarke, Eric Chitty, a Canadian, and, oh yes, an Australia, Charlie Spinks. England won 67 – 38.

When Jack did finally call it quits he retired to his home in Rugby and, according to reliable reports, became one of the sights of the town – an old man in flying scarf and Rockfist Rogan* goggles *(see page 88)* tootling round the area on a motorcycle.

But it wasn't quite over. On speedway's 50th birthday in February 1978 at Hackney organised by Len Silver, Parker took to the track again at the age of seventy-one. It was his speciality, a match race, and his challenger was the then England captain Malcolm Simmons.

Guess who won. Jack.

But, interviewed for this book Malcolm revealed. 'As for that race with Jack Parker, I can honestly say it was just "pleased to meet you Jack". Then Len pulled me to one side and said: "Would you mind letting Jack win? It will be really good for everyone if he did." Everyone except me, that is. As England Captain I also had an image to maintain. But reluctantly I agreed and that's how it ended.'

The real Parker swansong, his final appearance before a speedway crowd, came a decade later at the Golden Greats meeting at Coventry. The Parker brothers – Jack and Norman – were driven round the Brandon track in an open car. He had been away from speedway then for an astonishing 34 years, but he threw wide his arms in salute to the fans on the packed terraces, who responded with as great an ovation as was given to any of the other legends on view that day – Ove Fundin, Barry Briggs, Anders Michanek, Ivan Mauger.

He had them, as he always did, in the palm of his hand.

Jack died in St Luke's Hospital, Rugby on New Year's Eve 1989 after a hip was broken when he was hit by a car outside his home. He had developed pneumonia. A six line paragraph recorded his death in the *Daily Mail.* It read: 'Speedway rider Jack Parker died in hospital in Rugby aged eighty-four. Parker captained England on several occasions.'

It was a meagre requiem for a man recognised throughout the speedway world as *the* finest speedway rider England has ever produced. And it has always been a travesty of justice that he was never summoned to Buckingham Palace to be knighted for his services to the sport.

I was with him on his last ride, and I swear he was a record breaker to the end. He took it in a hearse on the way to Cranley Crematorium, Coventry. I had followed the courtege along the Dunchurch Highway and had the devil's own job to keep up.

I have absolutely no doubt whatsoever that Parker, Prince Of Cinders, had a celestial chuckle over my predicament.

They laid his silver helmet among the flowers at his funeral – and his well-worn old white scarf with the one word – JACK – said it all.

NORMAN – THE GREAT INSPIRATION

THERE were four defining moments in the speedway career of Norman Parker. The first was Thursday, 7 March, 1946, the day the speedway establishment – promoters and administrators – went into a huddle at Control Board headquarters to pool all the talent there was available.

The idea was to equalise team strengths as far as possible before the beginning of the sport's new awakening, when big time league racing resumed after being halted by the war. Wimbledon's astute boss Ronnie Greene chose Norman to lead his Dons. And Norman, to begin with at least, was not best pleased about that.

The second defining moment was Thursday, 22 September, 1949, the first post-war staging of the official World Championship Final at Wembley. It was the night that Norman, after two straight wins, had convinced himself that he would be England's first World Champion. It wasn't to be.

The third defining moment broke the sequence. It was Monday, 9 June, 1952 and the first Test of the season against Australia. Norman was captain of England that day on his home track, Wimbledon. In the very first heat he and Jack Young clashed on the first turn. The result for Norman was a fractured skull, England lost 56 - 52 and he did not ride again that season.

The fourth and final defining moment came the following year and was back in the old routine, a Thursday, during the second leg of the National Trophy final at Wembley. It was to bring the final curtain down on Norman's racing career that had spanned 24 years – and this time he went out in a blaze of glory.

But to get the full picture of the legend of Norman Parker, we have to go back even further than 1946, to 1915 when as a six-year-old he was growing up in Birmingham with his younger brother, John, or Jack as he came to be universally known.

In one of a limited edition series of 1s 3d autobiographies called *My Story*, Norman's references to his brother border on hero-worship. The reason: Little Johnny Parker had saved Norman's life by snatching him from beneath the wheels of a speeding motor car, becoming so badly knocked about himself that in later life he always looked all elbows when he raced a speedway bike.

A family affair: Jack presents Norman with his own trophy at Southampton in the very early thirties. Looking on is promoter Jimmy Baxter (in the hat) who is credited with 'saving speedway' by introducing team racing which led to the formation of the leagues.

Still together, the brothers move on to Lea Bridge. From left, Wally Lloyd, Billy Dallison, Norman, Jack (on the bike) Phil Bishop, Roy Barrowclough and Alf Foulds.

Jack began his track career in 1928, Norman a year later in 1929. Then they both rode for Coventry, and until the war they appeared in identical race jackets. Norman lived and raced in the monumental shadow of Jack, the garrulous crown prince of speedway. Jack had glamour and flamboyance, the charisma that went with world stardom.

On the track the Parker brothers were inseparable. When Coventry closed they went to Southampton, then to Lea Bridge Clapton and finally to Harringay until the war put a stop to almost everything. But even then they were among the gallant band who kept the sport alive through the dark days at the famous We Never Closed meetings at Belle Vue – at the old Hyde Road place, that is.

And Norman was always happy to play second string to Jack. Until Ronnie Greene made him a star in his own right on Thursday, 7 March, 1946. There was precious little major talent around, because the pre-war Australian and American big names who were not resident in Britain stayed at home that first year after the war.

Demonstrating his dominance for Wimbledon post-war, Norman in distinctive action with Harringay's Geoff Pymar in close attendance.

Is that hero-worship in the eyes of the young men listening to the wisdom of veteran Norman? They are his Wimbledon protéges New Zealanders Barry Briggs (left) and Geoff Mardon.

So it was, when the motors roared back to life, the big time returned and even bigger crowds flocked to stadiums throughout the land, ushering in a new sporting golden age, that Norman Parker took his rightful place amid speedway's elite. And he turned out to be not only wise but as steady as a rock and twice as reliable.

Looking back, that single event almost certainly was responsible for the way modern speedway is today. Norman Parker's authority and tuition moulded and inspired the rare and precious talent that was the young Ronnie Moore who he discovered in New Zealand. Ronnie's success inspired Barry Briggs who inspired Ivan Mauger. And Ivan Mauger inspired just about everyone who came after. There cannot be a more dynamic chain reaction than that.

In 1946 six teams were involved in the premier division, the National League, the equivalent of today's Elite League. They were: Wimbledon, West Ham, New Cross, Wembley, Belle Vue Manchester and Odsal Bradford. Six riders were designated as Stars and each promotion chose one on the lucky dip principle, making up the remainder of their teams in turn.

The stars were: Eric Chitty picked by West Ham, Ron Johnson picked by New Cross, Bill Kitchen picked by Wembley, Alec Statham picked by Odsal and Jack Parker picked by Belle Vue. Norman went to Wimbledon.

He said: 'It didn't please me too much when they split us up in 1946. But if Jack was the great individualist, I wanted to be the greatest team rider. I don't know if I consciously thought it, but it may have been my way of establishing my own personality.'

Three years later, a day of reckoning of sorts presented itself during that first post-war World Final at Wembley. Coming up to the interval there were three names on the leader board with two wins each, Tommy Price of Wembley, the eventual winner, Jack Parker and Norman Parker. The brothers had both proved the master of pre-meeting favourite Wilbur Lamoreaux of America.

Early sponsorship: Norman endorses Goodyear tyres.

They lined up in Heat 13 alongside the Australian pair Ken 'White Ghost' LeBreton and the Blond Bombshell, Graham Warren. With Lammy out of the way, Norman had been told by his pit crew that the title was his. And the way he had been riding he was, more importantly, convinced of it himself.

But he remembers coming out of the first bend 'with it all on' and seeing the figure of Jack ahead of him. Norman said: 'There was only one way to pass Jack, you had to go underneath him hard and shift him out of the way. I just couldn't do it. I had to shut off.'

But, on speedway's night of nights, with his confidence so high and the title virtually within his grasp . . . why did he back off?

'Because winning the world title meant so much to Jack, that's why,' he said. 'If Jack hadn't been in the race I would have won it.'

For Jack there was always a barely concealed matter of bitter regret that the official title always eluded him. In his seven World Finals he came closest in 1949, runner-up to Tommy Price at the age of forty-one.

For England there has probably never been an international track partnership to equal, let alone rival, that of the Parker brothers. Norman always hesitated to place their understanding as high as telepathy, yet he was never far from admitting it was so.

It earned them a formidable reputation as an opening Test team pairing for England, in Britain and Australia. Yet, as their contemporary international Reg Fearman remembers, there was never any love lost between them when they raced each other for their respective league sides.

At the end of the 1947 season Norman was nominated to challenge for Jack's Pension, the Golden Helmet British Match Race Championship, at which Jack so excelled. Norman won the first leg at Wimbledon, Jack won the second at Belle Vue. The decider was set for New Cross on 1 October.

Speedway News magazine reported: 'Norman took the first heat in brilliant fashion, giving the impression he would finish up champion for his time was only 0.6 secs off the track record. Heat 2 was packed with thrills . . .'

Top sports columnist of the day, Peter Wilson, star man at the *Sunday Pictorial*, the competition's sponsor, reported on the high drama that followed. He wrote: 'Norman went off like a house a-fire and never gave Jack a chance in the first heat. The two brothers were battling desperately for position on the third lap of the next heat when, suddenly, Norman was seen to be in difficulties and fell heavily on the back straight.

'Jack completed the extra circuit and then ran to his brother's aid, for it was seen that Norman's leg was jammed in the wheel of his machine.'

Brotherly love and the special understanding were left at the starting gate when Jack's Belle Vue met Norman's Wimbledon. Here they are in opposition during a league match at Hyde Road.

The famous Golden Helmet match race decider in the gloom of New Cross in October 1947. Promoter Fred Mockford is about to toss a coin to determine starting positions. It all ended in disaster for Norman and Jack kept the Pension.

The infamous Jack Young Incident which Norman never forgave. He is closed down by Young as they go into trurn one of the opening heat at Wimbledon in the first Test of the 1952 series. Norman, riding with a steel brace supporting an injured foot, high-sides and is about to crash. The crowd was extremely hostile over the accident and it virtually ended Norman's racing career.

Norman was trapped in the bike for twenty minutes and at one point the fire brigade was called to help free him. But as the drama unfolded, former World Champion Lionel Van Praag – the Nicki Pedersen-type hard man at the time with whom Norman, and others, had had numerous confrontational moments – had crawled under the bike and was supporting it across his shoulders to take the weight off Norman's trapped leg.

Lionel had ignored the hot exhaust pipe searing into his racing leathers and it left him with a nasty burn across his back. It was an example of another kind of speedway brotherhood. Against advice Norman, typically, insisted on taking part in the deciding race on a borrowed bike, but he was in no condition to win and Jack retained the Golden Helmet.

By 1952, after more than two decades of racing, Norman was a veteran. Brother Jack, the unrivalled choice for the captaincy of England, had been badly hurt in a midget car crash in Australia during the winter. So Norman was made skipper in the first Test of the season against the Aussies at Wimbledon, though he was riding with an injured left foot in a special steel brace.

Norman, with his Wimbledon team mate Cyril Brine, faced Jack Young and Merv Harding in Heat 1. Disaster struck at the first turn. Young dived between the England pair onto the white line, shut the throttle on Norman who ran into his back wheel, high-sided and was thrown awkwardly into the fence.

As the partisan crowd gave vent to their feelings and booed Young, Norman was on his way to hospital with a fractured skull. It was a bad accident, especially for a man in his mid-forties. He didn't ride again that season and he never forgave Jack Young for what happened. Interviewed about the incident, he said it was a more or less unwritten rule among speedway riders that you did not close down a following opponent as Young had done. 'He should have known better . . . ,' was Norman's verdict.

For Norman, who originally set out to be a carpenter, it had always been a hard road to follow Jack. But against his father's wishes he decided to take to the track as well. His first attempt scared the entire assembled company.

Jack explained to him how to broadside and then Norman was let loose in a race against

The 1948 speedway elite line up at Wembley for the grand parade before the Speedway Riders Championship Final. From the left: Bill Gilbert (out of picture), Eric Chitty, Jack, Bill Longley, Ron Johnson, Oliver Hart, Wilbur Lamoreaux, Norman and eventual winner Vic Duggan. In the second row: Frank Hodgson, Split Waterman, Alec Statham, Lloyd Goffe, Dent Oliver, Malcolm Craven, Jeff Lloyd and Ernie Price.

the old Stamford Bridge and Wimbledon star Gus Kuhn. Norman was all over the place, on the grass, sliding round lamp posts, bouncing off the fence. It was an out-of-control, crazy performance which had track officials and pushers-off running for cover.

For the last three laps of the race the red stop lights were winking furiously and of course Norman took no notice. He eventually steadied down enough to earn a place alongside Jack in the Coventry team and was proud enough to invite their mother along to see him ride. He treated her to his usual flat out, harum-scarum style and got back to the pits to see his mother being carried away in a dead faint.

What can perhaps be considered Norman Parker's finest hour came in the year following the Jack Young incident in the second leg of the 1953 National Trophy final against Wembley at the Empire Stadium. Norman's doctor had told him to take things easy, so he was not the force he had been and had dropped right out of the World Rankings. Only five years earlier he had been third behind the great Vic Duggan of Australia and Wembley captain Bill Kitchen, placing him one above bother Jack.

The Dons took a 28 point first leg lead with them to Wembley. It had been achieved, said Norman, by completely disorganising the Lions at Plough Lane. Wimbledon had been told to forget their famous team riding efforts and go out for themselves and Wembley had been unable to cope.

At the Empire Stadium the home side steadily pulled back the points and the crunch came in Heat 17, with the Dons relying on their old warhorse of a captain and the very young and inexperienced New Zealander Barry Briggs to clinch it for them.

Norman remembered: 'Before we went out Barry said to me: "Come on, Skip, I want to win this so that I'll have enough money to go back home this winter." So instead of going out to do my usual potter, I go out to win.

'I go shooting into the first corner just like I used to, look over my shoulder and see that poor old Barry is last. That was no good, so on the pit corner I shut them in and Barry had enough sense to know what I'm doing – that's why he became such a big star. He'd got it. Anyway, he came through into third place and away I go again. And that's the way we finished. I win, Barry's third and we win the trophy.

'But I began to realise that it hasn't done me any good. The crowd was very pleased and

Norman bows out in triumph: 11 September 1953 and 40,000 people see him inspire Wimbledon to win the Daily Mail *National Trophy final at Wembley. An obviously far from fit Norman accepts the trophy from R.A. Redhead, the* Mail's *general manager. Joining in the celebrations, Barry Briggs, Peter Moore, Reg Trott, Ted Brine (manager) Cyril Brine and Ronnie Greene (promoter).*

people started to throw me up in the air. But I'm not feeling very well.' Norman's great victory was a storybook ending to a great racing career. After the meeting he collapsed on the way home and never rode again, though he later went on to manage Swindon where he renewed his association with Barry Briggs who by then had become a multi World Champion.

Briggs has said: 'Maybe Norman didn't quite have the ability of his brother Jack, but I liked him better. He was certainly an inspiration to me as a sixteen-year-old in New Zealand. He was very good at knowing what was going on. He was really down to earth and though he may not have had Jack's talent he did things his own way.

'He went out of his way to help young riders. If anything he was too nice and he suffered because of that, especially when he was my team manager later at Swindon. I mean, some of the guys need their cages rattling sometimes.'

CHRIS AND DARCY . . . PURE AND SCARY

THE nearest the modern era has had to a pairing approaching anywhere near the remarkable Parkers' on-track understanding were the Americans Billy Hamill and Greg Hancock. Today it is the Australian partnership at Poole of reigning World Champion Chris Holder and the precocious but undoubtedly talented Darcy Ward.

The closest to them is their team manager Neil Middleditch, who says of their team riding exploits: 'They normally have a discussion before a race. They know their opponents pretty well and can often read what they are going to do, and if a certain situation arises they are prepared to counter it.

'As you know, I have been in speedway all my life and in my memory cannot ever recall a better pairing. The scary thing is they are still young and there is more to come from them.

'They are pure box office, and wherever we go people are in awe of some of their moves. I have stood with other riders at meetings and even they can't believe some of the moves they pull. I think, as you say, they are almost telepathic sometimes because often they don't even have to look for each other.'

Chapter 6
TERMITE'S TRAVELS . . .

THEY do things differently in America. Especially when it comes to speedway. They are much more – er – laid back. There is a fantastic amount of razzmatazz.

Stop me if I'm wrong, but I think the Yanks coined the phrase 'a whole new ball game'. Speedway, of course, is not a ball game . . . but you probably get my drift.

I had the great good fortune to experience first hand speedway Southern California style at a time when there seemed to be a regular production line of ready made stars lining up to bring their undoubted talents to Britain, and Europe: names such as Autrey, Penhall, Schwartz, Cook, Sigalos and the Morans readily come zooming out of the past to remind me of what, I suppose, was a vintage era for American, and world, speedway.

They were glamorous, they were articulate, they knew how to communicate and they cared what visitors like me thought about their quaint little rodeo ring circuits and indeed the fabulous racing they produced.

They could put on a show, those Yanks. Almost as good as the Poles do now – but idiosyncratically different – and light years away from the funereal atmospheres you get at so-called Elite League meetings in Britain these days.

Anyway, there I was on a Wednesday night at the National Orange Showgrounds at San Bernardino – a beautiful name which, for some unfathomable reason, the locals shortened to San Berdoo. It was known as the Inland Motorcycle Speedway and, around those parts, it really was *The Only Reason For Wednesday Nights* – a slogan which was, as I recall, appropriated soon afterwards without so much as a by-your-leave by Poole speedway.

The pace was frantic, the girls were gorgeous, the scenery – fabulous snow-capped mountains and trackside palms – sensational, and the racing, the climate and the Mexican food were hot, hot, hot.

Everybody who was anybody in US speedway turned up at San Berdoo on Wednesday nights.

They told me that the speedway rider I was watching had a wooden leg. They said they had a nickname for him: it was Termite. And then they clutched their sides and fell about laughing.

The sceptical Limey in their midst of course didn't believe them. He thought they were *having a larf* at his expense. I thought they were pulling my British leg and invited them to pull the other one because it had bells on.

No, no, they said. It's true, he really does have a wooden leg.

Now I'd heard of a speedway rider with only one eye, Alec 'Farmer' Grant who rode for Newcastle in the late 1940s. They called him Farmer because that's what he was when not racing. He'd lost an eye in a farming accident, but they let him carry on riding.

I also knew of a speedway rider with only half a foot. Mike Beddoe of Bristol, the result of a crash at Fleetwood in 1948.

And I'd heard of a speedway rider with only half a brain: former England and Wimbledon star Bob Andrews who emigrated to New Zealand and told me: 'New Zealand speedway suggested I apply to become a Kiwi, so I had half my brain removed and became one. This allowed me to race for New Zealand and I became captain of the New Zealand Test team.'

Most famous of all, of course, was the speedway rider with only one thumb, ironically an American, Jack Milne of New Cross and the first of America's World Champions to win the title in 1937. Jack had a thumb sliced off by the West Ham safety fence. The missing digit was found in the Custom House silver sand and handed back to him in a matchbox

Been there . . . done it all: seven times National US Champion Mike Bast, in casual mode on the bike, seems to be offering Dave DeTemple the benefit of his vast experience.

. . . or so the legend goes *(see page 80)*.

So, back to Termite, whose wooden limb appeared to be a bit of a hoot to my hosts, but to him it was certainly no laughing matter. Termite's real name was Dave DeTemple. At the time he was nineteen and was beginning to be noticed by the international speedway pundits. Another candidate for England – or so everyone thought.

Dave's Dad was thrilled to bits with his son's progress. He'd had him on a bike since he was almost three, even though he had been born with a short leg – the right one. Eventually they decided to amputate just below the knee and fit a wooden limb to kind of even things up a bit. He was never in the least embarrassed about discussing it and it seemed to make no difference to his track performances. He could thread his way through from his back mark, taking the occasional tumble on the way, with the best.

Once, in one fall, he broke his wooden leg. He said: 'I got hooked up on another rider's bike. And Bobby Schwartz told me that if that ever happened I should wind up the throttle and break free. Well, I did that and came down in a big heap. When they picked me up my wooden leg was broken. 'So my Dad straightened it out, made some splints out of a couple of tyre irons and I went right back out and rode.'

Dave's big ambition at the time, naturally, was to follow his buddies to Britain. So on his behalf I asked the British authorities if there was anything in the rulebook to say he would be refused permission to ride. The AC-U verdict was: 'It is likely that he would be asked to agree to an examination by a doctor who knew about the game. If he was given the OK he would be allowed to ride.'

Well, you didn't have to be a Johnnie Hoskins of a promoter to realise the crowd-pulling potential/publicity value in having a star rider with a wooden leg in your team, did you?

Dave DeTemple did come to England. He stayed at my house and we went to Reading one night where he was introduced to the crowd with a trip round the track on the grader. But, guess what . . . his leg fell off.

It was his thing, you see. He used to do it on purpose to cause gasps of astonishment from the paying customers.

But Dave DeTemple – Termite – never did ride for an English team.

I've always wondered why?

The real function of Orange County: Termite out on his own at Costa Mesa.

Chapter 7

PEERLESS PLECHANOV

By OVE FUNDIN (Five times World Champion)

I THINK Igor Plechanov has been overlooked. All of the Russians when they first came to race were very reserved. They weren't allowed to talk to us. Of course I met them quite early before they came to England.

I met them in Poland. It was the first time I got to talk to them a little bit. When I say talk to them I didn't know any Russian and they didn't know any Swedish or English.

I remember that I asked them to smuggle some bottles of whisky or vodka for me because I was sure the customs wouldn't search them. We were travelling together and I bought a few bottles and put them in one of their trailers. There was no problem and then I gave them a bottle as a gift for doing it. I still remember they drank the whole bottle in no time at all. They were all quite heavy drinkers. And they drank the pure vodka in big glasses.

Igor was a hard rider but he was fair. He beat me twice in the World Championships. In 1964 in Gothenburg I had beaten him in Heat 20, which meant we were both on 13 points. I made a good start and managed to hold him off for almost four laps, but he came past me fast on the last bend

He did it by overtaking me on the outside, a risk I wouldn't have taken. I could have

The magic of the man from Ufa: Igor Plechanov being chased by England's Nigel Boocock.

drifted out a bit to close him off, but I didn't. He never gave up. It was very difficult to do that to me, but he did it. He thought I'm going to get him and he put everything on. He came on the outside and he knew I wouldn't fence him. What he did was then described as the greatest ride that didn't win a World Championship.

He did it again, almost exactly the same, the next year at Wembley. We met in Heat 16 and I beat him, and if he had won that race he would have been in a run-off for the title with Bjorn Knutsson. But I won it and again we ended up on 13 points each. Then he made a better start than me in the run-off to finish second and I was third again.

And of course I remember just after the Russians had ridden their first Test match against Great Britain at Wembley in 1964, they came to ride against my team at Norwich – but only four of them turned up.

There was Plechanov, Gennady Kurilenko, Gabdrakman Kadirov and Yuri Chekranov. And they beat us 55-53. They rode nine times each and Igor scored 19 points. They were absolutely fantastic, and the Norwich supporters loved them.

Plechanov's team became so popular during the series that the British Speedway Riders association had a special diploma made congratulating them on their sportsmanship.

Igor was a particular fan favourite because he was a keen badge collector and liked to swap with supporters. He was reported to have collected 75 badges alone on one appearance at Belle Vue.

In those days when the Russians were riding in Europe, they were not allowed to wear civilian clothes. They had to wear a sort of track uniform and they were not really allowed to talk to us. It was in the time of the old Soviet Union and they always had a minder with them.

In 2002 I was with Igor Kalashnik in Chisinau in Moldova and we were talking about Plechanov. I didn't know if he was alive or not, but Igor said he was in contact and suggested that we should send enough money for Plechanov to come to Chisinau so we could meet up. The money came from me, most of it from me, and a little bit from Kalashnik. It was quite costly because Igor came by train from is home in Ufa and he told me it took him three days.

When I came back to England and spoke to Reg Fearman we decided to try and get Plechanov over to England. We got together enough money to fly him and his grandson. I think I gave about £60 and everybody gave the same and we got together enough money and also that they had some spending money.

Then I met him again in Chisinau with Boris Samorodov and he gave me his Hero Of The Soviet Union diploma. It was a big thing, because he was Sports Hero Of The Soviet Union a couple of times. The diploma was all in Russian of course, with lots of stamps and lots of signatures on it.

When I asked him what he was doing Igor told me he trained young motocross riders – not speedway riders, motocross riders. At the time he was made a Hero Of The Soviet Union he had a very good pension. But when the Soviet system collapsed in 1991 the money was worth almost nothing and he later got a job in charge of a go-kart track.

Fan favourite: one supporter shows how much she likes Igor.

Leading the invading Red Army: Igor at the head of his team on the grand parade before the first Test between Britain and Russia at Wembley in 1964.

High class opponents . . . and friends: Ove Fundin and Igor Plechanov at Mallila in 1967. There had to be mutual respect for them to get this close.

No favours. On the track it was strictly business, as Igor leaves Barry Briggs in no doubt about his winning intentions during a Great Britain v Russia encounter at Sheffield in 1965. On the far left Clive Featherby and on the far right Yuri Checkranov.

There is no question he is the best Russian so far. Today Emil Safutdinov is very good but he is not in the same class as Igor was. Of course not. Igor may have had a bad night at the World Final in Malmo, but remember it was his first World Final, which is always difficult for everyone. But he was always up there in the top. All the Tests that we did in Sweden and England he was always the top scorer.

It will take some time until Emil can do the same thing. He is very up and down. He started like a rocket, but he's very young. And a bit wild, where Plechanov was very, very steady. I can't think of any time that I saw him fall off. I have never heard anyone say anything about him that he has fenced them, or cheated them in any kind of way. He was a very nice and clean rider. He was very popular everywhere.

Above: *World number two: Igor (right) having won a run-off for second place with Ove Fundin (left) for the second time at the 1965 Wembley World Final. Racing driver Jim Clark does the honours for the new speedway World Champion, Sweden's Bjorn Knutsson.*

Left: *The master of kidology, a long-retired Jack Parker could be trying out his psychological tactics on Igor before a Test match at Coventry. On the far left is pre-war English international Squib Burton.*

We rode together in Austria, we rode together in Poland and various places and he was always very popular. He was always smiling. Like most of us, not least myself, we get quite angry, you know, and not so happy looking when everything doesn't go our way, but he was always smiling.

THE MISSING BIKES MYSTERY

SEVERAL speedway machines belonging to Russian riders disappeared on the night of the 1972 Wembley World Championship Final.

Tony Clarke, a more than useful rider with West Ham, Wembley, Newport, Wimbledon and Wolverhampton, subsequently went to jail for dishonestly handling three stolen JAWA speedway bikes plus spares belonging to the Russians.

In a recent interview with *Backtrack* magazine Clarke readily admitted: 'Yeah, I nicked 'em.' He said that visiting Russians would bring with them not only entire machines and engines but also other equipment to turn into Western currency.

He is quoted as saying: 'I didn't have the money to buy it from them, so I thought f**k it, I'll help myself – simple as that.' Involved with him were his brother Terry and a friend named Ben Griffiths whose van they used.

According to Clarke it was all stored in a garage belonging to his brother in what he described as 'a lock-up' near the stadium. There was a police swoop on the premises and they were arrested and eventually he was sentenced to fifteen months in prison. His brother was later given a three-year jail sentence for another offence.

Former Wembley captain Bert Harkins remembers the incident that night well. He recalled: 'I had parked my car with my JAWA on the back outside the Wembley pits and when I came back there were a couple of burly Russians taking my bike off of the bike rack! It was explained to me that their bikes had gone missing so I agreed to let them ride mine.

'Unfortunately, this was the bike involved in Briggo's crash where he lost a finger and my bike went flying over the fence. The frame was bent and I finished up riding the track spare in my next meeting.'

There were six Russians in the 1972 World Final: Alexander Pavlov, Viktor Trofimov, Valeri Gordeev, Viktor Kalmykov, Amatoli Kuzmin and Grigori Chlynovski.

From the start of the meeting there were on track incidents in races involving them. Chlynpvski was in Heat 1 which had to be re-run three times. In Heat 2 a brilliant tapes to flag win by Barry Briggs took the wind out of Ivan Mauger's sails, but he met with disaster in Heat 5 in a clash with Sweden's Bernt Persson. It resulted in hugely spectacular mayhem on the first turn in which, after colliding with the fallen Briggs, Gordeev's machine somersaulted over the safety fence.

It was the end of Briggs's bid for a fifth world title. He was taken to hospital where surgeons were unable to save a badly damaged finger. And the bike which leaped the fence was Bert Harkins's.

Igor Alexandrovich Plechanov

Born July 26, 1933 in Ufa, died 1 August, 2007. He finished second in the Speedway World Championship in 1964 and 1965 and was USSR National Champion in 1960, 1963, 1965 and 1968. He also coached the USSR national team from 1970 until 1972.

World Final appearances
1961 - Malmö, Malmö Stadion - 13th - 4pts
1962 - London, Wembley Stadium - 10th - 7pts
1964 - Göteborg, Ullevi - 2nd - 13pts
1965 - London, Wembley Stadium - 2nd - 13pts
1966 - Göteborg, Ullevi - 8th - 8pts
1967 - London, Wembley Stadium - 4th - 12pts
1968 - Göteborg, Ullevi - Reserve - Did not ride

Gesture of friendship. The special diploma from the British speedway riders congratulating Igor and his men on their outstanding sportsmanship.

Time to contemplate: Igor surveys the scene before an England v Russia meeting at Wolverhampton in 1966.

I was saddened to learn of Igor's death in *Speedway Star*. I was fortunate enough to have seen Igor ride during his prime. Here are a few personal memories.

Igor was the first good Russian rider to become known in the west, and arguably their greatest.

Those old enough may remember him for his smiling face, almost enough to melt the cold war, and his friendly disposition – here was a great ambassador.

I believe he first became known in 1961. I first saw him at Wembley, in the first test match with USSR. The Russians were not that strong, but they were great triers. However, Igor, and Boris Samorodov were genuinely world class. Igor was twice runner up in the World Championship, no mean feat in the one off WC days, when you did not ride regularly in the west.

Igor's style was all action, rather like that of Barry Briggs, and he was VERY GOOD INDEED. Almost a veteran in terms of age he was, for five or six years, a true superstar.

I have seen it suggested that he could not come from the back. This was not true, in my experience he was very good at it, and did it most of the time. Igor tried 110%, always and I think there can be no doubt that, had he ridden for a UK team, he would have won the title more than once. In the days of Briggs, Fundin, Knutsson, etc., this man could live with the best.

Perhaps my best memory is when dear old Norwich, ever keen to get one over on the rest, decided upon their own test match, Norwich v USSR. Unfortunately, the 'powers that were' vetoed this at the last minute, and allowed only four Russians to appear.

Offered a best pairs event, the Russians elected to race the Test match format, each riding in every other heat throughout the evening. It was great racing. 18 heats, Plechanov, Chekranov, Kurilenko and Kadirov two, then two, with no reserves to call on.

Igor scored 19 points, plus a fall while racing Olle Nygren, in his 9 heats.

Fundin scored an 18 point maximum, Nygren got 17, Hedge 9 and Bales 8.

Kurilenko got 16, Kadirov 9 and Chekranov 9, none had been to Norwich before.

In 1964 not many people beat Nygren around Norwich, but Igor took that point from Olle. The score, USSR 55, Norwich 53........in what turned out to be Norwich's best ever year in the top flight.

Believe me, this smiling, badge swapping racer was one of the true speedway greats.

Thanks for the memories Igor.

The final resting place: Igor's son Igor (left) and daughter Veronika at the commemorative graveside they erected in their father's memory.

Chapter 8
YOUNG AUB AND HIS MYSTERY CHAPERONE

THEIR TRUE ROMANTIC STORY

YOU wouldn't be far wrong if you said that Aub Lawson was an overnight sensation. After only two years racing experience in Australia he was allowed to travel to England – accompanied by his sister to hold his young hand – and in his first season he qualified for the World Championship Final.

Only two other riders in the entire history of speedway racing have reached a World Final in their first season. Ronnie Moore and Jimmy Rexton.

Well, no. That's not strictly true. 'Red Hot' Jimmy Rexton (*see page 87*) was really a fictional character and therefore didn't actually exist, so Ronnie is the only one.

Aub Lawson, the young Sydney telegraph delivery boy, started his speedway career in 1937, making an immediate impression with his flamboyant leg-trailing style and his long scarf billowing out behind him.

He made such rapid progress that he was selected for the Australian side in the Test series against the England touring team at Sydney in the 1938-39 season, riding in four of the five matches. The company was fierce and definitely world class. Aub's Australian team mates included the reigning World Champion Bluey Wilkinson, Lionel Van Praag and Vic Huxley. In the England side were Jack and Norman Parker, Arthur Atkinson and Alec Statham.

The great Van Praag, World Champion in 1936, who was captain of the Wembley Lions at the time, saw the potential in Aub and invited him to England for the 1939 season. It has always been accepted that Aub, then twenty-five, travelled with his sister Joyce as his

On duty: a youthful Aub Lawson during the war on active service somewhere in the jungle.

'chaperone'. That is not strictly true either, but it is such a heart-rending human story that we will reveal the truth behind it all in good time.

Joyce, who is now ninety-three, has throughout the years kept secret the real reason why she 'chaperoned' Aub during their trip to England for the 1939 English season. But through her daughter Betty and Aub's daughter Rosemary she has at last revealed the amazing untold story.

Joyce's recollections, as told to Betty, are these:

WHEN Aub was invited by Lionel Van Praag, on behalf of Wembley Stadium, to go to England, he asked his younger sister Joyce to accompany him. Aub was three-and-a-half years older than Joyce, but they were great mates. Even though she was already very keen on a young man, David Cossill, Joyce was eager to travel overseas. On 3 April, 1939 she celebrated her nineteenth birthday on board the *Orcades* on their way to England.

One disappointment for Joyce occurred on the very first day of the voyage when her new watch, a farewell present from workmates, was stolen from her drawer while she was showering.

Aub's trip to England was financed by Wembley Stadium on the recommendation of Van Praag, but their mother paid Joyce's £100 fare. Jeff Martin, Aub's mechanic, accompanied them at his own expense.

They thoroughly enjoyed life on board ship for the six week duration of the voyage. The speedway riders, who were all heading for different destinations, were a very sociable group. Joyce recalls her surprise at the on-board romances that even the married speedway riders engaged in, but Aub always kept a close eye on his younger sister.

Short of funds, Joyce and Aub's activities at various ports of call were mainly restricted to walks or tram rides. Sometimes Aub contacted the local scouting association who gave them a warm welcome. When Aub and Joyce first arrived in England, they were taken into the home of the manager of Wembley *(at that time Alec Jackson)* until they organised a flat of their own in Wembley. This was to remain Aub and Joyce's base throughout their stay in England.

Aub's speedway career was a little slow to progress. Initially he was given very few opportunities to ride at Wembley, and had to compete at less renowned speedways in country areas.

(The 'country' speedways referred to must mean the Second Division and Middlesbrough, to whom Aub was loaned. But Middlesbrough didn't last the season, even though crowd figures are given as 22,997. Their record was expunged. Aub rode in three matches scoring a total of 25 points for an average of 8.33, a promising performance for a newcomer. He is listed as being returned to Wembley in May, though is also listed as being on Middlesbrough's 1939 retained list and not on the Wembley list.)

Start of the big adventure: Joyce and Aub surrounded by well-wishers about to embark for England.

Far left: *Having the time of their lives: Brother and sister on board ship.*

Left: *Champion escort: Speedway's first World Champion Lionel Van Praag, the man who arranged the trip, poses with Joyce during the voyage.*

The speedway fraternity on deck making the most of the long sea trip. Taking the air are Aub (far left), Joyce, Lionel and on the right Charlie Spinks and Wally Lloyd.

Joyce recalls that their means of transport was an old car that nearly asphyxiated its occupants with fumes, so that journeys were interrupted by frequent stops to clear the air.

To begin with Joyce worked at Wembley Stadium on the dog racing tote, but she often accompanied Aub when he competed at country speedway venues, and she later obtained a job as a comptometer operator in Finchley to help with expenses.

Aub's successes at country speedway venues meant that he was given more frequent opportunities when he was recalled to ride at Wembley. In a few months he progressed to the point of being selected to ride in all five Tests against England and being among the qualifiers for the World Championship Final. It was little short of sensational.

[*Aub, fellow Wembley team mate Malcolm Craven and veterans Frank Varey (Belle Vue) and Eric Collins (Wimbledon) all reached the Final with four bonus points. They were in the company of such top liners as former champions Jack Milne (see page 80) and Van Praag together with America's Cordy Milne (Southampton, see page 84), Arthur Atkinson (see page 26) and the emerging Vic Duggan (Wimbledon).*]

The overnight sensation: Aub in his Wembley sweater on a visit to Belle Vue in 1939.

Life in the speedway world at Wembley was extremely exciting. Aub coped very well with the celebrity aspect of his growing popularity and Joyce enjoyed the attention given to her as Aub's sister. There were always parties after race meetings, although Aub and Joyce were not drinkers. Aub quickly became the subject of adulation, and he often used his sister to fend off his more enthusiastic female admirers.

Joyce remembers a darker side of the speedway world at Wembley. The best riders received the most money according to a points system for first, second and third in competitions. Aub considered that there were elements of dishonesty around the system for assigning starting positions in races. Stewards could manipulate the outcome of the draw so that a rider would receive an advantageous position on the track. In addition, some riders had the drive to win at all costs, even when it involved endangering the lives of others.

Aub had always intended to return to Australia after his contract with Wembley Stadium expired, but Joyce had planned to explore the Continent while she had the opportunity. However, all of their plans, including the World Championship, had to be abandoned as the threat of war loomed.

As the likelihood of war increased, Aub and Joyce became eager to return to Australia. Aub wanted to enlist with his friends in Australia and Joyce was keen to return home to the family. Because many of the ships of the Orient Line were commandeered for troops, it became a waiting game to obtain a ship's berth. As people became more anxious about the likelihood of bombing in London, Joyce was encouraged to go to Peacehaven near Brighton with Lionel Van Praag's wife Gwen and her sister to await news of a ship to Australia.

One of the highlights of this short period in Peacehaven was the proximity of the popular singer Gracie Fields. Joyce recalls being disappointed that she did not recognise Gracie after sitting next to her on a bus. When Joyce later sent a note of apology and admiration to Gracie, she was rewarded with a kind note from Gracie that Joyce still has in her possession nearly 75 years later.

Still awaiting news of a ship, Joyce went up to the Scottish border to relatives of Aub's mechanic, Jeff, and Gwen returned to London to be with Lionel. Finally, in October, 1939, Aub and Joyce obtained a berth on the *Oronsay* and travelled back to Australia around the Cape Of Good Hope because the Suez Canal had been closed. Joyce remembers the nightly blackout conditions and thinking how ineffective the single gun mounted on the back of the ship would be in the event of enemy attack. During the war Aub distinguished himself as a Signals rider and Joyce served in the WAAF.

AND that wonderful human story . . . Rosemary writes:

'Nanna Lawson was not being overprotective of Aub in 1939. There was a reason she sent Joyce with Dad. Not only were they great mates but Nanna was being overly protective of Joyce who had fallen in love with David Cossill at nineteen, and she thought the trip overseas would cool the romance.

'However David went to war, was captured in Crete and imprisoned in Stalag 13 for the duration. Joyce did not know whether he was alive or dead, but she waited and when he was eventually released at the end of the war they married. I was at their wedding as a

Testing time. Riding as partner to his Wembley captain and mentor Lionel Van Praag (right), Aub chases England's Alec Statham during the third Test at Harringay in 1939. All of his soon-to-be-familiar unique style is there and his eight points helped Australia to a 58 – 48 win.

Hammering around: Aub (outside) and Wally Green show the opposition a fine piece of team riding at Harringay after the war.

Star captains: Aub, leading Australia, and Jack Parker, leading England, wait for the coin to drop before choosing starting positions before a Test match.

Planning the downfall of England: Aub and the great Vic Duggan.

young child. They were together for more than sixty years and became the Darby and Joan of the era.

'They have created a dynasty of numerous grandchildren and greatgrandchildren. There was a party when David was alive for his ninetieth and Auntie Joyce said it was a wake so that all their friends could be together and party while they were alive. I cherish that we still have Auntie Joyce for many years yet in good health.'

AFTER the war, Aub resumed his speedway career in England and became one of the sport's biggest international names with West Ham and Norwich where, as he had been introduced to Wembley by Van Praag in 1939, he introduced Sweden's Ove Fundin who went on to win five World Championships.

Of all the old pre-war stars, Aub was the most enduring. He qualified for the last of his ten World Finals in 1960 at the age of forty-four. His best finish was a third place to Barry Briggs and protégé Fundin in 1958.

He died in 1977 at the age of sixty-two and is buried in Karrakatta Cemetery, Perth, Western Australia.

Chapter 9

TRIUMPH AND TRAGEDY

THE TOM FARNDON STORY

AT THE AGE of twenty-two he had reached the very top of his profession. He typified the unquenchable spirit of adventurous youth. No film star had such a devoted following. He had won every speedway championship there was to be won. At one point in his meteoric career he held all the National League track records. He was, at the time, probably the best speedway rider in the world.

As if he had not been blessed with gifts enough, he was also devastatingly handsome, superbly spectacular and magnificently consistent. He was said to possess the perfect combination of skill, judgment and daring.

The destiny of Tom Farndon (England, Crystal Palace and New Cross) was surely to become the greatest speedway rider England would ever produce. And it is as certain as anything can be in this crazy speedway business that he would have brought the individual World Championship title to England a full thirteen years sooner than did the magnificent Tommy Price of Wembley.

But on the night before what promised to be another of his regular finest hours, tragedy of the utmost magnitude – and certainly of monstrous perfidy – struck him down.

Going like the clappers at Clacton: Tom ahead of Vic Huxley.

Throttle jockey: Tom kicking up some dust at New Cross.

He was then twenty-four years old, and though his achievements, up until fate turned its cruel ferocity upon him, had bordered on the monumental, his future potential appeared limitless. Tragically he was never to realise the full promise of his unique abilities.

Tom Farndon really liked horses, and he originally thought he might like to be a jockey. Riding motorcycles started out as just 'a bit of a lark'.

But he could not have had a finer speedway apprenticeship . . . riding with the Parker brothers, Jack and Norman *(see pages 30 to 46)*, in his home town team, Coventry. It was a very short apprenticeship. He and the Parkers parted company when Coventry closed in 1931, the brothers going to Southampton and Tom to the Fred Mockford-Cecil Smith metropolitan promotion at the truly spectacular Crystal Palace.

From then on his fame rose like a comet. His wild and precocious speedway talent refined itself into what we now know as superstardom.

But to his big sister, Hylda, he was her baby brother. Before her death Hylda enjoyed life in some style in Leamington Spa, Warwickshire. It was there, looking down as the spring blossoms began to carpet her local park with colour, and surrounded by her scrapbooks, photograph albums, newspaper cuttings and her memories, she talked to me about 'Our Tom'.

'He was lovely,' she said. 'He was dead keen on horses and used to go to the local blacksmith's. He was very young, but he used to ride the big shire horses. He fancied being a jockey, and one racehorse owner took him on for a month to see how he liked it. But he didn't care for racehorses as much as the shires.'

In one of her cuttings, under the headline *'Daredevil lad who won speedway fame: How Tom Farndon led his father a fine dance'*, a 'Special Correspondent' has written: 'He was a crazy, fearless young daredevil. So mad, so hot-headed, that his father, a downright, plain-speaking coal merchant, would not let him ride a motorcycle.' The reason: Dad feared his son would break his neck. The Special Correspondent wrote that 'Tom Farndon, the speedway ace, had fair, curly hair and passive blue eyes behind which there is a hint of quiet strength and a steadfastness of purpose, but there is certainly no suggestion of recklessness'.

He used to pull bikes to pieces and reconstruct them. Then he started experimenting with motorcycles belonging to friends. He never lost an opportunity to sneak off for a joyride. He had plenty of spills – and father had to pay.

In the end he wore down his father's resistance and Farndon senior bought him a bike. So when the new speedway opened at Brandon, young Tom was one of the first through the gates. And here is where the 'bit of a lark' came in. That's what Tom thought it would be to try the new sport.

No easy ride, even at practice. Going for it are Tom (outside), Harry Shepherd (centre) and Stan Greatrex.

He stripped down his machine for practice sessions and, mounted on his improvised speedster . . . he crashed! He crashed more often than any of the others. He never got round two laps without a crash, according to a Special Correspondent.

Then, one afternoon, a director of the track lent him a proper speedway bike, a Dirt-Track Douglas. First time out on his new mount he beat the previous night's best times. He was only two-fifths of a second off the track record. At this point, says Hylda, he was spotted by a local motorcycle dealer by the name of Stanley Glanfield. Now Stanley Glanfield just happened to be *the* Stanley Glanfield who, by chance, had been traversing the globe in a motorcycle combination about the same time as Lionel Wills. They both seemed to end up in Australia just when dirt track racing was beginning to take off as a national pastime. It was their reports of what they saw that resulted in the birth of speedway racing in England. The deal was that Mr Glanfield would supply a machine in return for a share – a goodly share according to Hylda – of Tom's winnings. She says: 'Mr Glanfield wanted so much money when Tom won that my husband, Joe, said: "Forget that!" and bought Tom a speedway bike of his own.'

'First time out he crashed. He wasn't hurt much, but the trouble was the handlebars. Tom had very short arms and they couldn't find suitable handlebars for him. But eventually he got to the stage where he was very, very good. Then the track went bust and he went to Crystal Palace. He didn't like the big Palace track, he liked the tricky little tracks. That's why he was such a success when Palace moved to New Cross. It was small.'

It was around this time that Tom met and married a Coventry milkmaid, Audrey Gledhill. They met at a dance, recalled Hylda, but Tom was so shy that he would never ask any of the girls to trip the light fantastic. So Joe used to say to him: 'Tell me which one you want', and he would make the introductions. Audrey was also shy, refusing to be married in a traditional white wedding gown in a church ceremony because she didn't want any fuss. Yet, although Tom was supposed to be shy, Hylda said: 'I remember he won a Charlston competition at the Coventry Hippodrome and the prize was a clock. He seemed to be pretty good at whatever he did. And when he became a really big speedway star in London, he used to be mobbed wherever he went. He had to be smuggled in and out of places the back way – just like modern pop stars.

'The big stores used to borrow his trophies to display, and he never had to buy anything to wear – it was all given to him. He was treated like a major celebrity. But it didn't seem to change him. I remember him one day racing against Syd Jackson. Tom beat him and Syd threw down his bike afterwards and said it was no good, he couldn't win on it. Tom bought it off him on the spot and went out and won on it straight away.'

Off the track Tom developed an interest in racing greyhounds, at one point owning 14 of them. Hylda said: 'The first we knew about it was when Dad bought the *News of the World* and in it was a picture of Tom jumping over a fence with two dogs. When Tom was killed, I had his best dog and it literally earned me a fortune over the years.'

Our Special Correspondent refers to Tom having a track career marked by an 'almost unbroken run of triumph. Here are the highlights: Farndon is the only rider who has ever held the National League Riders Championship, the London Riders Championship and the British Individual Championship simultaneously; he alone has successfully defended the BIC twice.'

The Special Correspondent forgot to mention that Tom had also won the prestigious Star Championship in 1933, from his team mate Ron Johnson and West Ham's Bluey Wilkinson.

But it was far from an unbroken run of triumph. For instance, when Fred Mockford and Cecil Smith signed him for the Palace, they soon found that he was not altogether the success they had hoped. The reason was that he tuned his own motors. It was said that they used to employ a special member of the track staff whose job it was to walk round the circuit and pick up the parts that fell from Tom's machine.

Things changed when the team moved to New Cross, where Mockford and Smith introduced the track workshop system, under the mechanical guru Alf Coles, where the machines of the entire team were looked after. It is reported that from then on Tom Farndon didn't have to worry about a mechanical thing. He never saw his machine until an hour before a meeting. He went out and raced, and then forgot about his bikes until the next meeting.

There was controversy too. It was early in 1935 that a £25 best-of-three challenge match race series was organised between Tom, the reigning British Champion, and Bluey Wilkinson, the Australian Champion, and very likely Tom's next opponent for the national title. It was an event obviously designed to 'pack 'em in' almost certainly cooked up by Mockford and his old Docklands 'enemy' Roarin' John Hoskins, for both were old-school showmen speedway promoters in the true sense of the word. OK, 'Old pros' if you like.

Historian Cyril May reported: 'The New Cross ace sky-rocketed round the big West Ham circuit to victory at the record-smashing speed of 45.68mph, which was 0.68mph

Hey, that's my Dad: Tom's son Roy perches on the family limousine to oversee his father's mechanical skills.

Still speedway life: Tom with the New Cross London cup winning side before a meeting at Belle Vue. From the left they are: George Newton, a mechanic, Stan Greatrex, a mechanic, Tom (leaning on the bike), Joe Francis, Harry Shepherd, Roy Dook, a mechanic, Mike Erskine. Only captain Ron Johnson is missing.

better than the old record established by Vic Huxley in May 1934.' (So Tom Farndon could ride the big tracks well after all.)

By all accounts though, the two promotional gentlemen concerned neglected to inform the Speedway Control Board about their enterprise, so the Speedway Control Board put its collective foot down, forbidding the match to take place in the style of the official British Individual Championship, and ordering the riders to meet for one race only at each track. They reasoned that such an imitation as had been planned would, of necessity, detract from what was then the principal competition of the day.

And inexorably, the career of Tom Farndon moved towards its destiny.

The 1935 speedway season had hardly begun when Tom Farndon set up a new track record at New Cross, and in so doing became the first speedway rider to complete four laps of a track in less than one minute.

In June he fended off the challenge of Hackney's Dick Case for his British title. By then he had worn the crown longer than any other rider. Such was the standing of the competition at the time, that New Cross supporters chartered 22 motor coaches to travel to cheer on Tom in his deciding match against Case at Wembley.

His remarkable form made him favourite for his next target, that year's Star Championship at Wembley, the final of which was due to take place on Thursday 28 August. Both the British and the Star championships involved the elite of world speedway who treated the paying public to the finest and most spectacular exhibitions of individual racing. The Star finals were, in effect, really the unofficial World Championship Finals of the day.

On the night before the final – the Wednesday and New Cross's usual race day – the Rangers, who were lying second in the league, met Harringay who, led by Tom's former Coventry team-mate Jack Parker, were on a winning streak. Depleted by the absence of the injured Joe Francis and Harry Shepherd, New Cross lost. Tom contributed nine points and won his second half scratch heat.

Cyril May was there and described what happened: 'I still have vivid recollections of the evening, the New Cross Scratch Race Final, with Tom, Stan Greatrex and Ron Johnson (all of New Cross) and Bluey Wilkinson (of West Ham) taking their places on the starting grid.

'Remember, Ron and Tom had virtually carried the team for several months; they were, in less than a minute, put out of action at a single blow.

'From the tapes Ron and Tom took a slight lead, but fewer than two yards separated Ron's back wheel from Tom's front. More than a little halfway down the back straight on the third lap, the New Cross skipper touched the fence and fell. So close was Tom that there was never the slightest possibility of his avoiding the crash or laying down his machine.

'Tom and his machine were thrown into the air, and he was flung an incredible distance before falling on his head. It looked from the terraces as if Tom deliberately turned, to try and hit the fallen machine instead of the man.'

Audrey was among the thousands of fans who saw the crash. Both riders were taken to hospital. Ron Johnson escaped serious injury – no broken bones, but he was badly bruised and had severe lacerations to an arm. It was enough to keep him from the following night's Star Final at Wembley. But Tom's injuries were far more serious.

The entire incident had been witnessed by Bluey Wilkinson, the fourth rider in that fateful race, who said later that he had sensed 'something was going to happen' and had deliberately stayed out of the way. Bluey, of course, was also in the following night's Star Final, and may well have decided on a prudent approach to what was, after all, an unimportant race compared with the big night to come.

The *Speedway News*, in its account of the meeting, reported that 'Wilkinson finished alone....' His time: 63.8. The race had been re-run and Greatrex had pulled out after being 'filled up'. The accident was recorded – in small type – on page 12 of that edition. *A Black Night For New Cross*, was the headline, and the report read: 'Last Wednesday night was the culmination of the blackest period in the history of New Cross speedway or, for that matter, of London Motor Sports Ltd. At the Miller General Hospital, Greenwich, Tom Farndon fought for life for 48 hours. Newspaper reports told of amazing scenes outside the hospital. Hundreds of women prayed in the pouring rain.'

Such was Tom's following that regular bulletins on his condition were posted on the gates. Tram and omnibus drivers stopped their vehicles at the hospital so that their passengers could read the notices. Two days after the crash Tom died without regaining consciousness. By ten o'clock that evening the crowds – including hundreds of weeping women – had grown so big at the hospital gates that police had to be called to control the multitude. Many of Tom's female fans had collapsed when his death was posted and had to receive medical attention. Several vowed they would never visit a speedway track again. One said 'Everyone loved Tom Farndon. He was such a wonderful rider and one of the cleanest and most unspoilt stars of the tracks.'

The eulogy in *Speedway News* ironically reported Tom as saying: 'If I ever have a serious crash I shall retire.' He was, said the feature, 'perhaps the most colourful rider of his day . . . the harder the race the better Farndon liked it, nor was he wont to make an excuse on the rare occasions when he had to acknowledge defeat. The limitless adulation he received

Grief: surrounded by solemn fans, Audrey stands with bowed head at Tom's graveside and views the huge wreath in New Cross colours.

Top left:
Homage to their hero. The huge crowd which gathered on the New Cross terraces to pay their last respects to Tom whose coffin has been placed in the middle of the centre green.

Top right:
Pall bearers carry Tom's coffin away from the stadium, his helmet on top of the casket draped in the New Cross flag.

Above left:
The speedway world mourns. Floral tributes on display from other clubs.

Above right:
Overwhelmed: the enormous amount of flowers that were placed at the grave.

when a mere youngster would have turned most heads, but Farndon remained modest and unassuming to the last. No champion of any sport has ever worn his laurels so gracefully.'

THE *full Tom Farndon story is in the book* Tom Farndon: The Greatest Speedway Rider Of Them All, *by Norman Jacobs and John Chaplin*

THE LEGEND LIVES ON . . .

THOUGH Tom has been gone seventy-eight years, he may not be entirely lost to this world. Some years ago his ghost was reported to have been seen by a young Loraine Tedds in the cemetery where he is buried. Loraine grew up in Coventry but now lives near Scarborough. This is her first-hand account of her disturbing experience:

'IT MUST have been a summer Saturday when it happened. Because we often went swimming in the summer months. My brothers Gary and Brian, a friend, Johnnie Price, and myself all decided that if we walked alongside the railway track we could get to the swimming pool just as quickly as if we had taken the bus, but even better, the money we saved on bus fares could be used on extra sweets.

'On our way home we were busy making small talk, laughing and giggling, recalling events of that day's swim, when as we were walking on the part of the embankment that ran alongside St Paul's Cemetery we were stopped in our tracks by the loud noise of a motorcycle engine coming from the cemetery.

'We turned to glance over at the graveyard and to our amazement saw a motorbike with a rider in the middle of the graveyard path revving and revving the motorbike. The rider was just revving and revving the bike while looking in our direction. I couldn't see his face clearly as he had on a full-faced helmet. The helmet, as far as I can recall was kind of metallic silver/blue. The rider was wearing all black and the motorbike was black, but a very shiny black which in the sunlight shone and glistened.

'As children we had never seen any motorbike or rider looking such as this, the only motorbike and riders we had ever seen were always just plain black bikes with the rider having "Gerry-type" helmet and goggles.

'So to see such a bike and rider as this was really scary. In our child minds we thought this must be one of those Hell's Angels that we had heard about but never seen.

'The image was very clear. It was a sunny afternoon, around I would think 4pm. How long we stayed there mesmerized and glued to the spot I don't know, maybe only seconds but it seemed like ages.

'Suddenly the rider dropped his clutch and the bike started heading our way. Instantly we all just ran and ran as fast as we could, jumping over a barbed wire fence to get home even quicker. My brothers and I were all much taller then our friend Johnnie and we had no problem clearing the fence, but Johnnie couldn't jump it and had to scramble on hands and knees under the wire.

'We were too afraid to wait for him.

'My brothers and I continued running till we got home. We promised each other never to tell our parents because we would have been in trouble for walking alongside the railway and also for spending our bus money. That night in bed, because I was still scared, I told my sister Patricia all that had happened. Days later Johnnie came round to see my brothers and told them that he had run home crying because while he was trying to get himself unstuck from the wire he heard a smash and heard screaming and he thought the rider had got out of the cemetery and was coming to get him.

The girl who saw a ghost: Loraine Tedds and her brother Gary at the age when she experienced the graveyard apparition.

'A few days after the incident Patricia came home from school all excited and told me that they'd had a ghost story for the last lesson that day and the teacher told of a motorbike rider who was killed in a race and his motorbike was buried with him in St Paul's Cemetery, and that on the anniversary of his death people had witnessed a bright light going around the graveyard and heard the sound of a motorbike.

'Was it the legendary Tom Farndon we saw? I do know that the image I saw was as clear and as solid-looking as any living thing, yet it shone and glistened more brightly than I had ever seen before.'

LORAINE *went on to say that after discovering Tom's name she scoured the internet to find out as much information about him as she possibly could and said: 'I want to thank you and all the people like you who take the time to put pictures and information on the Internet because with your help I have discovered just who my ghost rider really was, the great legendary Tom Farndon. May his soul rest in peace.'*

Whatever the truth about Loraine's remarkable experience, the legend of Tom Farndon lives on.

Anniversary tribute: Loraine and the author at the gathering to comm- emorate the 75th anniversary of Tom's death in 2010 . . . it was a paranormal- free occasion.

The constant fan 75 years on: The lovely lady who said Tom was her girlhood idol and wanted to connect to the good times with a hands-on nostalgic experience, touches the uniquely beautiful art deco headstone on Tom's grave. Below and to the left is the small brass replica the author had specially made.

THE MEMORIAL

THE TOMBSTONE on Tom Farndon's plot at Foleshill Cemetery, Coventry, is remarkable. In beautiful smooth black marble, it is an art deco sculpture of a speeding motorcyclist and one of the most striking memorial stones in the country.

For years it was surrounded by the mystery of how it came to be there, who commissioned it and who made it.

Until a cutting was discovered from an issue of *Motorcycle Weekly* either in the late 1970s or early 1980s which reveals that the paper's technical artist, Lawrie Watts, having seen the headstone, contacted an old established monument makers in Coventry and sought out their oldest employee.

Watts discovered that Audrey, determined Tom should be properly remembered, commissioned the image from a sculptor named Richard Ormerod.

According to Ron Clarke, formerly senior keeper of visual arts at Coventry's Herbert Art Gallery and Museum, brothers Richard and George Ormerod were professional sculptors working in the city between the wars. They also designed a number of car mascots. Richard died in 1979 aged 83.

It took a while for Audrey to overcome a certain ecclesiastical reluctance, but she was finally given permission for the monument to be placed on Tom's grave.

For any speedway enthusiast it is well worth a visit. Foleshill cemetery is known as St Paul's Burial Ground and is located in Holbrooks Lane, Foleshill, Coventry. The grave is easily identified, it is just to the right of the chapel straight down from the cemetery entrance.

However, if you happen to be of a nervous disposition, take care when visiting. You never know, you may have a similar experience to that of young Loraine Tedds and her brothers . . .

Chapter 10

MEET THE MASTERS

THE WORLD CLASS ACTS BEHIND THE CAMERAS

WHILE Alice was having her *Adventures In Wonderland,* she thought: 'What is the use of a book without pictures or conversation?' Which is exactly what I was thinking when I began to put this book together.

When it comes to speedway racing, a picture of it is indeed worth many thousands of words. Well, it's an action sport. OK, an *action-packed* sport then. Anyway, though over some several decades I have written thousands – maybe millions – of words in my attempts to do justice to speedway racing, the value of those words has been enhanced immeasurably by the skill of the speedway photographer.

And so, I approached lots of speedway photographers and told them I would like to devote a special chapter to their important work. I asked them, if they would like to be featured, to send the picture they were most proud of, or which had the most significance for them, together with a few words telling the story behind the picture and some brief details of their career.

Nothing happened. The silence was deafening.

I concluded at first that maybe, old pros that they are, they had all decided it was a John Chaplin con, and that he was asking them to supply free pictures for his new book with little or no effort on his part. And then it occurred to me that maybe I was guilty of undue and uncharitable cynicism. Perhaps they were all rather busy at the time.

Whatever.

Eventually I went directly to two master photographers who I respect and whose world class work I have admired over the years. They are:

Mike Patrick, my long time friend and journalistic colleague who, until poor health forced him to realize it would be wise to give up the speedway treadmill, was acknowledged to be the world's leading speedway photographer.

Scott Dalosio, a Californian who has specialized in capturing the elbow-banging glitz of American speedway for many years, and also a long time friend.

***

Mike Patrick

ALL my aunts and uncles used to go to speedway, to see Vic Duggan and all these old names. They went to the London tracks: Harringay, New Cross, everyone went in those days.

When I was six years old my father took me to Wimbledon and I just loved it. It was that year, 1950, when I saw Ronnie Moore's first ride for Wimbledon. And from the moment I saw him I was on at my father to take me every week. Sometimes my sister would take me, until I was old enough to go on my own. I loved it. That's how it started.

Then girls and guitars sort of took over – I played guitar and was lead singer in a group. The comedian Freddie Starr joined us but we got rid of him after about three months because we thought he was holding us back. He was a good singer, but he wanted to do a lot of comedy stuff. So we let him go.

I didn't go to speedway. I was in a pop group, and we used to go to Germany, Denmark, Italy – all over. One time we went to Hamburg, went to the promoter's house and he said

Dear old pals . . . going back a long way: Mike Patrick, with the camera and his hero Ronnie Moore, in the famous Dons race jacket, a couple of ageing superstars remembering Ronnie's first ride for Wimbledon.

he wasn't expecting us for another month so we had to drive all the way back home again. No money. So that's when I gave up.

Then I learned photography – a friend of mine was a freelance professional photographer and he used to photograph musicians for a music magazine for living. And I said to him: 'Oh, I wouldn't mind doing that. Would you teach me?' He lent me a camera for about three months, then I took a postal course, and that was it. I blagged my way into a professional dark room. *Give me a chance . . . see what I can do.* And got a job in a commercial studio.

But I knew I didn't want to take photographs of weddings, landscapes or children. After about two or three years, not knowing which route to take, I went to a speedway meeting at Wembley in 1970. I saw a photographer running around on the centre green, and thought: *Ah, that's what I want to do.* I was full of it. When I got home, unfortunately my wife of that time had gone to bed. I lay awake all night planning it. I was going to go to Wimbledon . . . everywhere. I couldn't wait to tell her. And she said: 'Oh, no, not another scatterbrain idea.' I said: 'Oh yes I will and I'll be bloody good at it.' Forty years later I am still a speedway photographer and she is no longer Mrs Patrick.

About 1973 I went on a lunchtime Johnnie Walker radio show, *Pop The Question*, and I started talking about speedway. Things progressed and I ended up being on every day that week. I was always known as Mick, but he started calling me Mike, and from then on I was known as Mike Patrick.

I wrote to Wimbledon and asked if I could go on the centre green, and they said I could if I could supply local newspapers and get them to print pictures. I think I got five local newspapers to take the pictures, and I also had to write reports. I'd never written a report in my life. So that's how I started.

I had a lot of opposition – an enormous amount of opposition – from a well established top photographer at the time. He tried to get me banned by the British Speedway Promoters Association (BSPA) when I began advertising colour photographs.

I was up all night printing them and I approached some top riders, riders such as Christer Lofquvist and Terry Betts, and said do you mind if I take a picture of you, advertise it in *Speedway Star* magazine and you sign the picture? Yes, they said, no problem at all. I'd give them a tyre or two and give them photographs.

Suddenly I found I was up for being banned. It was being discussed at a BSPA meeting. I rang up the chairman, Reg Fearman, and he said: 'All the money you are getting through *Speedway Star,* the fans are not spending it at the tracks, you're costing us money.' So I had to promise to be a good boy and not advertise my pictures in *Speedway Star* any more. That lasted until there was a change of BSPA regime.

There was a move in speedway at one time by riders demanding a percentage of the money being made from the sale of their photographs.

The former World Champion Billy Hamill tried that once with me and I said fine, if I gave you ten percent from what I make from you in a year it would be about a tenner at the end of the year – if that – if I'm lucky.

So that squashed that, but if they wanted to stop me taking pictures, that was fine. I had this with Ole Olsen at first because he was so well in with Alf Weedon (whose slogan was *Established 1947*). Ole wouldn't look at me for a picture.

Another thing with Alf. I went to my first World Final, 1972 when Mauger won it. I went to the Press Office and could hear Alf talking to somebody: 'Oh yes, people put a camera round their neck and think they're a photographer . . .'

Anyway I got a pass to go in, but Bill Kitchen (the old Wembley captain, then a machine and safety examiner) wouldn't let me past the pit gate onto the track. I think he'd been

Mike in action – and trademark check trousers – getting down to capturing a match race between Peter Collins (left) and Dave Jessup.

Hot and bothered, what some people will do for a photo: Mike smiles with relief after the ordeal was over . . . but of course it was all his own idea.

'spoken to'. Everyone else was out there. So I had to spend the whole of that World Final in the pits. Plenty of good pictures there, but the action was out on the track – the Barry Briggs crash and everything.

It just used to make me laugh because Alf was the first one to come to me for help with his camera – he seemed to have no idea what he was doing half the time. He'd say: 'What does this do, what does that do?' I had to watch him. I had a hell of a fight on my hands at first. He'd say to the boys: 'Look at the camera,' take the picture and then thank them very much and they'd all walk off because they wanted to go racing. He dominated. He absolutely dominated.

As speedway progressed the technology progressed. In some ways it brought a lot more work, in other ways less. It allows you to take a lot more photographs, to be more creative. Experiment with longer lenses, shorter focus and you get a more brilliant picture without wasting loads and loads of film.

When we went to Grands Prix, or something big like that, I was limited to about ten rolls of film which when you add it up with the processing over a year it's a lot of money. So you couldn't let that motordrive run too much, and you'd miss stuff. You couldn't help it.

Digital made a big difference. But then I'd come back from a Grand Prix with about a thousand pictures because I'd be taking about ten a second. Where once, in the old days with film, if I was supplying someone in Australia or New Zealand I'd have to develop them – you could be up all night – put them in the post and they would print them a week later.

With digital it was immediate, which was brilliant. It opened a lot more doors for me, with newspapers and magazines, but at the same time a lot of publications were in trouble financially and were having cutbacks and restricting the number of pictures they would take off freelances.

In the winter you had to make the money stretch. And the winter would go so quickly. People would still be ordering photographs for Christmas, I'd be able to get away for a couple of weeks in November, then you had just a few months before the Press days started at the beginning of March. There were just a couple of months when it was quiet and you could get up to date with filing and catching up with contacts that you couldn't do during the speedway season. It was a twelve-months-of-the-year job.

Bad health finally decided me to quit. Without realising, for six years I'd been carrying Myalgic Encephalopathy (ME) which causes persistent fatigue and is sometimes known as Chronic Fatigue Syndrome (CFS). I thought it was just old age, you know, but there I was carrying seven and a half kilos of cameras around for hours at a time during Grands

Prix and all the work that was necessary afterwards. I just exhausted myself.

You might be away covering a Grand Prix for five days so all the other work would pile up. In the end I was like a zombie. Really, I found I just couldn't do the job. It was well known I'd got ME, so I don't mind talking about it. There are many people who are worse off than me.

There were of course many, many high points through following the sport around so intimately for so long, I think one of the highest was that nerve-tingling feeling when they played the national anthem as Peter Collins stood on the rostrum at Katowice in Poland after winning the World Championship in 1976 in front of 130,000 people. I was a good friend of PC at the time. That was one of my favourite moments.

Scott Dalosio

Was introduced to speedway as a teenager by his father, a car racing enthusiast, while growing up in Detroit, Michigan.

The eyes have it: Scott takes a sideways look.

I DIDN'T really know what speedway was. I was always interested in sprint car and midget racing, but my Dad thought they were too dangerous as drivers were always getting killed. The first time I went to one a driver was killed and my Dad didn't want to go back.

In 1972, we went to an indoor flat track motorcycle race and they had a speedway demonstration. There was also a story in the programme about the famous Harry Oxley, the promoter at Costa Mesa speedway, California. Little did I know that eight years later I would start working for and become a friend of Harry's. I still have that program.

We moved from Michigan to California in 1974 and I went a few times with my Dad to the paved track car races, but found them boring. So, for a few years I didn't go to any races, but in 1977 I went to a midget race at the famous Ascot track near Los Angeles. I was always interested in photography so took my camera with me. That race hooked me and I was back every week. The following year I got a job as the United States Racing Club (USRC) midget racing organization photographer.

From 1977-79 I shot all types of racing from midgets, sprint cars, NASCAR, Indy cars and flat-track motorcycles. Then, early in 1980, I was at Ascot to photograph a sprint car race and out of the blue some guy asks me if I would be interested in shooting speedway at San Bernardino Inland Motorcycle Speedway (IMS) for *Cycle News* magazine. I said yes and he also asked me if I had ever written any articles. I hadn't written anything, but I still answered yes. He called me a couple of days later saying I had the job and told me to call the promoter, John LaDouceur and his sister Kay Moran. That call changed my life!

I shot full time at IMS in 1980 and occasionally at Costa Mesa and Ventura. In 1982 I ended up full time at Costa Mesa too.

By 1983, things had changed. I was now shooting speedway more than car racing and loving every minute of it. Made a trip to the UK in 1984 to shoot the USA v England speedway Test Matches. When I was not at the track, I did a lot of photographing of World Champion Bruce Penhall and his endeavors away from speedway, including shooting him on the set of the television series CHiPS.

The biggest year for me shooting speedway was 1985. There was racing six nights a week and I shot at least five of the nights and occasionally six nights.

That was the year I consider was the start of the real decline in American speedway. When Bruce Penhall quit in 1982 it took some of the wind out of American speedway's sails. However, 1985 saw the crowds shrink at most of the tracks. Midway through the year the promoters took action to save money by cutting the racing purse, forcing many riders to find full-time jobs away from racing. It meant that many were unable to ride at all the tracks and crowds became even smaller.

In essence, the move backfired. The sport was just not the same. The daredevil riding that made it so popular declined as riders did not want to risk injury while riding for less money.

At the end of the 1987 season, San Bernardino IMS closed and moved to Glen Helen. The new track was bigger and it never caught on. After one season there, LaDouceur got out of the business.

I continued photographing speedway, but in 1988 I also started announcing events. The racing was not as good as it had been and therefore the photography was not as good. I continued to cover events for *Cycle News* but in May of 1991 I met my partner Robin. It was far more enjoyable to be with her and I started taking time away from the races. I shot my last races that year.

In 1992 I announced speedway at Lake Perris and still covered it for *Cycle News* at Costa Mesa, but with a pen only. I put my camera down for the last time in 1991.

Do I miss shooting speedway? Thinking back to the early to mid-1980s, yes! After that, it was more like a job and I don't miss that part.

Every so often I think about getting a camera and having a go at it again, but then common sense returns and I drop that thought. I have thousands of images from back in the early days when I really enjoyed taking them.

THE ULTIMATE WHEELIE

Mike Patrick

IT WAS my idea. I wanted to get the ultimate wheelie shot for the front cover of a book, and to get it from an angle that no one normally sees. I knew Hans Nielsen well, we had a good working relationship from his time at Oxford, though I'd known him from when he first started in speedway.

We travelled around together to World Championship meetings, we shared planes and had been in the same hotels. You get a good relationship with a lot of riders that way.

I put the idea to him and he said, yes, no problem. I said I wanted to do it when the crowd was around to get a bit of atmosphere and it was done at a Bank Holiday meeting at Oxford against Reading – in the interval.

He may have done about ten laps to get it right. I lay flat on the ground and didn't have a lot of movement as he came towards me because I was on my elbows. So he'd come hurtling towards me and every lap I sort of shut my eyes. He got closer and closer every lap and I could feel the rush of air past my face.

Close call: The ultimate wheelie shot that took Hans Neilsen (on the bike) ten laps to get right. You can't see it, but Mike's eyes are closed . . .

He had to be precise. I was completely in his hands. I remember hearing the fans going: 'Oooooh, that was closer.' I signalled with my hands to tell Hans to keep going, keep going. Or he'd come up to me and say I'll put some more fuel in and do some more.

When I eventually looked at the pictures, I chose the very first shot that I took. There was always something with all the others. But that one just stood out, although he did get closer to me, it wasn't a wide angle shot.

Each lap I opened the lens up a bit. I was only 95 per cent happy with it, not 100 per cent, because he was wearing goggles that go dark. I couldn't see his eyes. If I could have seen his eyes, imagine how that picture would look. Ivan Mauger told me that just by looking at the rider's eyes you could tell exactly what he was thinking. But 95 per cent is not bad.

Another photographer, John Gainsford, took pictures of me doing it. And you could see how close Hans actually got to me. It was a very, very warm Bank Holiday and I remember afterwards I was sweating like a pig. Whatever it was, adrenaline, or whatever, after I'd finished I just broke out in a hot sweat.

Health & Safety probably wouldn't allow it these days.

AN EYE FOR DRAMA

Scott Dalosio
I DON'T have a particular favorite photograph, but I have a top five and this one is in it. The photo is from the 1988 US National Championship at Costa Mesa and shows Bobby Schwartz just ahead of Sam Ermolenko and Greg Hancock with Brad Oxley on the outside.

One of the things that makes this photo unique, and I never thought of it until someone pointed it out, all four have won US National Championships and it was very hard to get four National Champions of that era together in one photo at Costa Mesa, or any Southern California track for that matter.

This was due to so many of the champions racing in the UK. I also say to myself when I look at this photo, and I have never sat down and figured it out myself, how many total titles this group has won.

However, my favorite part of the photo is their eyes. Any photo that shows a racer's eyes is so much more dramatic.

All in a row: Scott's unique action study of four US National Champions, with Bobby Schwartz leading Sam Ermolenko and Greg Hancock with Brad Oxley on the outside during the 1988 final at Costa Mesa. None of them won . . it was Steve Lucero's year.

Chapter 11
JACK MILNE'S THUMB

Y OU WILL almost certainly consider what I am about to tell you a rather unlikely speedway story. But I am the man who found the man who found Jack Milne's thumb. Jack, the 1937 World Champion, lost his thumb at West Ham. And, fifty-nine years later, I found the man who found it.

First things first. We need to know how Jack came to mislay his thumb – and since you ask, it was the left one – also, of course, how he came to be in a position to do so.

Born in Buffalo, New York in 1910, the modest and unassuming Jack always gave the credit – or, as he once said, the blame – for his racing success to his younger brother Croydon, more popularly and universally known as Cordy.

The family moved to Pasadena in California where Jack experienced speedway close up as spannerman to Cordy. Inspired by his brother's success, Jack recalled: 'It soon came to the point where it was my turn to make the cinders fly.'

The pair of them began to make the cinders fly all over the world, and their abilities were noted particularly during their visit to Australia in 1935. The enterprising London promotion team of Fred Mockford and Cecil Smith at New Cross, who that year had

A pair of Jacks: Milne – there is definitely a left hand thumb there – and Parker before an early England v America match race.

tragically lost their star man Tom Farndon *(see page 64)*, heard that these Milne boys were
a bit special and brought them to England for the 1936 season.

An unseemly squabble then broke out among the top English promoters about the
newly arrived ready-made American stars. The Speedway Control Board decided that
New Cross would be too strong if both Jack and Cordy were allowed to ride for the same
team, so Cordy was directed to a new side at Hackney Wick.

Within weeks Jack was involved in a crash in which the thumb of his left hand was
sliced off. Jack Mine's thumb – or the lack of it – is one of speedway's most enduring
legends. Until practice day at Wembley for the 1978 World Final Jack Milne had been
merely a magic name to me. But that day I looked across the room in the old stadium's
Long Bar, where riders, Press and VIPs were all quenching their thirst, and saw him.

Awed as I was to be in the presence of one of speedway's glorious greats, I plucked up
enough courage to approach him and introduce myself. The first thing I did, of course,
was look for the missing thumb. Sure enough, it wasn't there.

So the legend was true.

The accounts of exactly how it came to be missing are as colourful as they are legion .
. . the crash into the West Ham fence, and strong men fainting when the digit was recovered
from the cinders of the track.

The po-faced *Speedway News* magazine reported it beneath the heading: 'Hard Luck
Jack', and the text revealed 'At West Ham last week, having had enough time to learn
something of our tracks, Jack gave a splendid account of himself in the first round of the
World Championship – only to be involved in an accident – none of his fault – which
entailed the complete loss of his left thumb.

'Those who should know, including one or two famous riders, assure us that this
should be no great handicap once the wound has healed. We sincerely hope this is so, but
we cannot escape the fear that a fine rider has lost some of his effectiveness and in any case
he seems to have been put out of the championship, at least as far as this season is
concerned.'

A goodly number of years ago I interviewed Jack beside the pool at his home in
Pasadena, which looked out onto the magnificent rugged vista of the Los Angeles National
Forest and the Sierra Nevada. We had discussed the missing thumb, of course. He
confessed that at the time he was concerned that the loss of the thumb would impair his
performances.

Apart from Jack, only one man knew what actually happened that day at West Ham,
and for fifty-nine years he had remained silent. Until I met him at the annual dinner of the

The US triple
whammy:
Americans take the
top three places in
the 1937 World
Championship,
second is Wilbur
Lamoreaux on the
left, Champion Jack
Milne in the centre
and third, brother
Cordy Mile on the
right. Once more,
the thumb that isn't
there is hidden
behind the trophy.

Past masters: Parade
of World Champions
before the 1978
Wembley Final.
From the left Tommy
Price, Barry Briggs,
Jack Milne – the
thumb is quite
plainly not there this
time – and Fred
Williams. At the
back Bjorn Knutsson
and Ove Fundin.

old Dirt-Track Riders Association.

During our casual conversation I happened to mention the saga of Jack Milne's thumb. It was then that he confessed and revealed all. He had been a trackraker at West Ham at the time of the accident and saw it all. He said: 'When Jack crashed I saw something on the track. I realised it was part of his hand, picked it up and dashed to the pit gates with it where someone put it in a matchbox and gave it back to Jack.'

Who was the mystery man who had carried the secret of Jack Milne's thumb for almost six decades? He turned out to be Vic Scales, for many post-war years the Birmingham team's brilliant mechanical maestro. Why had he kept the secret for so long? 'Well,' he said, 'no one ever mentioned it to me before.'

The loss of the thumb put Jack out of action for a short time, naturally, but it didn't prevent him qualifying for the World Championship Final.

He reached Wembley with, amazingly, the same number of bonus points, nine, as his brother Cordy who finished fourth. But Jack finished down in ninth place.

The style of a champion: Jack Milne in action for New Cross . . . and the left thumb is most certainly conspicuous by its absence.

The controversial bonus point system meant a rider took to the Final a percentage of his qualifying score – in all pre-war World Finals riders did not start equal on the night. So, the most important meetings of the speedway year were in effect handicap events – bonus points being added to a rider's final on-the-night score.

The paradox being that Jack's best pal, Bluey Wilkinson, though unbeaten on the night, finished third after Lionel Van Praag and Eric Langton ended with better totals. Van Praag winning an equally controversial run-off for the title.

The following year was different. Jack led all the qualifiers, taking to the Final 13 bonus points, one more than fellow American Wilbur Lamoreaux and Eric Langton and two more than brother Cordy. It was a night of triumph for the Star Spangled Banner, America taking the top three places, Jack winning the title, with Wilbur second and Cordy third.

In 1938 Jack finished second to Wilkinson with Wilbur third. By 1939 Bluey had retired and though Jack again qualified, Cordy was in such devastating form that he was the favourite to become World Champion. But the outbreak of war prevented the World Final from being staged.

Incredibly, Cordy's other claim to fame was that he had married a lady named Marie Van Schaack who, it is believed, used him to escape to Europe from her humble American origins. She left him to pursue a lurid career as the world famous burlesque stripper Lily St Cyr.

Lily was tried in 1951 for 'lewd and lascivious' performances and volunteered to take a bath in the courtroom to prove her act was tasteful. The judge declined her offer, and the jury declared her work to be 'art'.

She eventually had six husbands, as well as romances with film stars Orson Welles and Victor Mature, among others. Her philosophy was: 'What's the use of being beautiful if you can't profit from it?' She died in 1999 aged eighty-one.

Jack Milne never returned to race in Britain after the war. In the Sixties, when speedway had all but expired in America, he helped his former hired hand Harry Oxley import the Briggs-Mauger axis which saw the sport rocket to unprecedented popularity on the West

Jack Milne's racy relations: this is brother Cordy in fine form on the track . . .

… and this is Cordy's wedding to Marie Van Schaack …

… and this is the modest Mr Cordy and the demure Mrs Marie on a club day out …

… and this is the demure Mrs Marie Milne after transforming herself into the exotic burlesque performer Lily St Cyr …

… and this is the exotic Lili St Cyr in fine form relaxing between shows …

I'd like to thank my friend Kelly DiNardo for permission to reproduce the pictures of Lili which came from her book Gilded Lili and the Striptease Mystique *(Back Stage Books)*

Coast, eventually producing two double World Champions in Bruce Penhall and Greg Hancock, and the other title holders Sam Ermolenko and Billy Hamill, plus loads of other talent.

Jack sort of retired to the best of both worlds, his beautiful mountain home and helping Oxley to run the enduring home of American speedway, Costa Mesa. He could often be found still putting in the laps at a fair old lick – on the track grader. 'I like to do this,' he once said to me. 'I leave all the shouting to Harry. He likes to get out there in front of the people . . . he's just like Johnnie Hoskins.'

He never told me what he did with the 'spare' thumb they returned to him in the matchbox that night at West Ham.

Chapter 21

A BOY FROM BALHAM

WHO BECAME A GENUINE GENTLEMAN OF THE TRACK

HIS great, great, great, great grandfather was Master Of The King's Musick (*Musick is correct*). His great, great grandfather was chimney sweep to Queen Victoria.

The sublime to the gorblimey, you might consider. You might also be considering: Where is the speedway connection?

Well, the speedway connection is that lower down that august family tree another star name found himself earning a living among the cinders.

His name was Philip Manston Hart – otherwise known to legions of speedway devotees as Tiger Hart.

The Tiger's more esteemed ancestor, a composer who wrote eight symphonies and the song *Hearts Of Oak*, is buried in the crypt of St Paul's Cathedral. His name was Dr William Boyce who, to bring you bang up to date is, coincidentally, a distant relative of Craig Boyce, among whose claims to fame is decking former World Champion and Polish superstar Tomasz Gollob at a Grand Prix and who went on to manage the Australian speedway team.

If the name of the erstwhile chimney sweep to royalty had a name it does not appear to have been recorded.

No matter.

Even though Philip Manston Hart strove to pursue a cinder-stained career on the dirt-tracks of the world, he chose to elevate his sporting image to the level of cricket's traditional amateur practitioners who were called 'gentlemen' and were identified by their initials, as against the more common herd of paid professional 'players' who were identified by their full names.

So, when I first came across the Tiger's billing in the Birmingham speedway programme (cost: a mere six copper coins of the realm, or two-and-a-half pence in today's money) it appeared like this:

P.M. (Tiger) Hart

It proclaimed him not only a star – and he was a star, from the way he dominated races on the track, to the way he dressed off it – but of higher rank than your ordinary jobbing speedway rider, a true aristocrat of the track. Well, after all, he was captain of the Birmingham team.

At that time, 1946, he was unique. He was speedway's only Tiger in action. The even more famous Harold 'Tiger' Stevenson, pre-war captain of England and West Ham, had resisted the temptation to climb back into the saddle after the war. And no one had even thought of John 'Tiger' Louis.

To me, and the countless thousands who flocked to the old Birchfield Harriers Alexander Sports Stadium, Perry Barr, Birmingham – the same place where the present Elite League Brummies ride – Tiger Hart was not only a local hero, he was a swashbuckling legend.

Born in Balham, South London, in 1908, he set out on the the road that led him to speedway following, at the age of sixteen, a row with his father who refused 'point blank' to buy him what he described as 'a gleaming 1911, 500cc Bradbury' motorcycle.

Silverware for the Tiger: an early success at Portsmouth.

'I stormed off in high dudgeon,' said Phil (he wasn't Tiger then), 'to Australia House in The Strand and made arrangements to take a boat to Brisbane.' So in the time-honoured melodramatic fashion, he ran away to sea.

It was 1924 and speedway had hardly been invented. The Tiger recalled: 'I had various fortunes in Australia, working the first few years as a farmer's boy. With my meagre savings I leased a prickly pear block of land from the Queensland government, but the venture was a complete disaster.'

Then, one day, a passing motorcyclist saw him driving a tractor, stopped and tried to sell him a BSA bike. But he explained that he earned a mere £1.10 shillings a week and couldn't afford one. The man who failed to make a sale was 'Wizard' Frank Arthur, soon

A badly marked historic picture from 1938 when the Birmingham Hall Green Bulldogs took on an American team. From the right, identifiable faces are: Steve Langton, Malcolm Craven, Manuel Trujillo, Tiger, the two captains shaking hands, Les Bowden and Cordy Milne, between them Bob Lovell and behind Cordy Danny Lee.

to become one of Australia's top speedway pioneers and a world star. And, Tiger recalled: 'My meeting with Frank Arthur was eventually to change my life completely.'

The young man was conscripted into the army, the Australian Light Horse, which formed a guard of honour for the visiting future King George V1. 'That night, the local enterprising speedway promoter ran a meeting,' said Tiger. 'I went. It was the first time I'd seen a dirt-track, and from that moment it was all I ever wanted to do.

'So I started racing in 1927 at a place called Toowoomba. Three years later Steve Langton and I were spotted by Frank Arthur who had just returned from London. He recognised me and said: "You want to come to England, that's where the money is."

'I said: "We can't ride." And he said: "Neither can they."

'So Steve and I sailed for England, a 12,000 mile, six week trip with full board and lodging which cost £36.'

In London the two aspiring speedway hopefuls met pioneer Clem Cort who called Johnnie Hoskins at Wembley, who said: 'Send 'em over.' Hoskins fixed them up with rides at Portsmouth.

'They thought we were Australian and jumped at us,' said Tiger. 'At Portsmouth they had a publicity truck they sent around town with billboards on that announced: "Steve Langton and Tiger Hart." And that's how I got the name Tiger – they just dreamed it up.'

The misconception over his nationality was to see him ride for both Australia and England in speedway representative matches – until his Balham birth was finally established.

After Portsmouth he went on to King's Oak, West Ham, Plymouth and Hackney Wick, 'finishing up at Birmingham where I became a permanent fixture.'

He captained the Birmingham Bulldogs at Hall Green before the war, and when league racing restarted in 1946 he led the new Brummies at Perry Barr in the old Northern League, then the equivalent of today's Premier League.

The 1946 'New Brummies'. From the left: Charlie Appleby, Stan Dell, Tiger, Cyril Page, Roy Dook, Bob Lovell and Ernie Appleby (no relation to Charlie).

The side included old Hackney team mates Stan Dell, Doug Wells and Charlie Appleby, the vastly experienced Roy Dook and Bob Lovell from Bristol, plus Australian Laurie Packer from Glasgow – all men who had ridden with such greats as Bluey Wilkinson, Tom Farndon *(see page 64)*, Jack and Cordy Milne *(See Page 80)* and the Parker brothers, Jack and Norman *(see page 30)*.

To almost a man the 1946 Brummies were all leg-trailers, and became known as the Team Of Trailers. Only Tiger and Ernie Appleby (no relation to Charlie) rode in the modern foot-forward style.

'Just after the war I went with an ENSA team to Europe to entertain the troops,' said

Perfect pair: Tiger (inside) and his partner Bob Lovell delight the vast Perry Barr crowd with their special brand of the lost art of team riding.

Tiger 'I had a big job – I was Ron Johnson's minder . . . What a job.'

Johnson was the New Cross captain and a world star. But, revealed Tiger: 'You couldn't keep him away from the booze. One night in a Brussels hotel I was called downstairs at about midnight. "Mr Hart," they said, "Mr Johnson is trying to kill the hall porter." Ron had come in drunk, got into an argument with the porter and was trying to throttle him. When Johnno was drunk there was nothing he wouldn't do.'

In the early part of the 1946 season Tiger led the Brummies to the top of the Northern League table. But it didn't last and they finished the year fourth out of the six teams. In the

The 'permanent fixture' at Birmingham in 1947. From the left: Laurie Packer, Dick Tolley, Ernie Appleby, Bob Lovell, Roy Dook, Tiger, George Gower and Stan Dell.

Tiger with a rare collection of fun-loving Northern League stars at Bradford in 1946. The riders are, from the left: Fred Tuck, Wilf Jay, Len Tupling, Joe Crowther, Will Lowther, Tiger – who seems to have acquired a rather splendid trophy – Wilf Plant and Geoff Godwin.

knock-out National Trophy Birmingham were unfortunate enough to meet the first division National League champions Wembley, losing 80 - 27 at the Empire Stadium – Tiger top scored with 8 – and 77 – 31 at Perry Barr – Tiger top scored with 11.

He had an almost telepathic understanding with his race partner Bob Lovell, a hang-off-the-bike spectacular full-on trailer who complemented Tiger's more sleek and upright foot-forward style. Their team riding was legendary. And, though they were definitely Second Division, on 4 April, 1947 they were invited to London to take part in the grand gala reopening of First Division Harringay.

The opposition was definitely First Division: Ron Johnson, the man Tiger had tried to keep away from the bottle on the ENSA tour, and Eric French (New Cross), Norman Parker and Mike Erskine (Wimbledon), Joe Abbott and Norman Lindsay (Harringay) among other London top liners.

Contrast in styles: the spectacular leg-trailing Bob Lovell and Tiger combine to keep out the opposition.

Speedway Gazette reported: 'Of all the stars and near stars on view it was Second Division rider Phil Hart who set the track alight. The Birmingham captain did the seemingly impossible by coming from behind to beat Norman Parker and later had an easy win over Joe Abbott. Pity that Phil was a non-finisher in his other rides otherwise we might have seen a great scrap between him and Ron Johnson.'

Indeed we might.

It was not until 1948 when the phenomenal Blond Bombshell Graham Warren *(see page 144)* arrived at Birmingham that the club took on the gloss of success that projected it, as now, into the big time.

By then, Tiger had retired from the track. And, until then, he had never realised how popular Tiger Hart was in Birmingham. He began a car sales and insurance business that boomed thanks to his name and the speedway fans who flocked to buy and insure his vehicles.

For twenty-six years the Tiger had a home in Puerto Andraitx on Majorca. It was there, in 1995, a year before he died that we sat together in the sun by the side of the marina and talked. He was eighty-eight, was suffering from cancer and he looked frail, but he spoke for a long time about his life and times.

On these days of big moneyed intercontinental commuting speedway stars, it is interesting to compare the Tiger's pay sheet for a private booking at Glasgow in August 1947. He had six starts at £1 a start, scored eight points at £2 a point, and it was a 576 mile round trip (no motorways then) at three pence a mile, £7.4 shillings. That totalled up to £29.4 shillings (£29.20p). Deductions were 8 shillings and 3 pence for fuel, oil and insurance. Leaving £28.15s.9d (about £28.77.5p) for risking life and limb.

He said: 'In the early days, of course, big stars like Sprouts Elder were paid lots more. When I was transferred to West Ham, which Johnnie Hoskins was running for Arthur Elvin of Wembley, he used to pay us a 50 per cent bonus – in cash.'

And on money, he revealed what he claimed was the secret of what went on in the Wembley pits just before that crucial and much discussed Heat 19 at the 1951 World Final from which Jack Biggs needed just a single point to take the title.

'Jackie wanted one point from his last ride,' said Tiger. 'The others were saying to him: "Well, Jack, what about a tenner each to make sure?" And he said: "Look, I've won my first

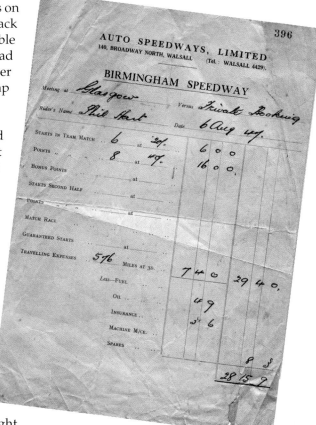

Tiger's pay sheet from a 576-mile round trip to Glasgow in 1947.

Accident-prone. Ambulance men are in attendance as Tiger, who is on crutches with a broken leg after one of his crashes, says farewell to Birmingham's end of season crowd. The helping hand belongs to his team partner Bob Lovell. Rider with his back to the camera is Dick Tolley.

four, I'll win this one as well."

'He was last.

'They were all looking for a backhander. It didn't happen. When riders had no chance of winning the meeting they would sell points. Today it seems to be: win at any cost. In my day there was more of a sporting attitude. There were also some vendettas – blokes looking for each other.

'I wouldn't decry speedway riders now – they are good. But I look back and think about that fabulous stadium at Perry Barr and think what we could have done then with sponsorship.

'After the war I rode for Les Marshall at Birmingham. He was a very lucky man. The crowds were enormous. But he used to pay every dime in Entertainment Tax (it was 48 per cent at the time). I tried to show him how to avoid it, but he insisted on paying. I went to Wimbledon in 1948 because I fell out with him.'

Graham Warren burst on the Birmingham scene in 1948 and later Tiger was the Brummies' team manager. He said: 'I don't think Graham liked me very much, but to me he was the greatest, fastest rider there ever was. Somehow he could keep a bike more upright and get more drive. He was fabulous. He was a cocky little sod, but that was part of his success.'

It was a persistent leg injury that forced the Tiger to give up racing, and even though his car sales business thrived, he never really left speedway.

Backing Hoskins at New Cross: Tiger, in his promoter's suit, and a rather self-satisfied looking Johnnie Hoskins on the right. Peter Craven – in unfamiliar New Cross race jacket – has just been presented with the trophies for winning the Tom Farndon memorial meeting by the late Tom's brother Syd.

'I managed Tamworth for two years, then became manager at Perry Barr until it closed in 1957,' said Tiger. Two years later he and the Old Warhorse Hoskins re-opened New Cross. 'I had been in the South of France, and when Johnnie called me to say he'd got New Cross, he said: 'We'll make millions, but I haven't got any money. If I can say you're my backer – my partner – I'll be OK." '

But the co-promotion partnership didn't last long. Tiger said: 'When speedway came back to the greyhound stadium at Perry Barr in 1971 I became clerk of the course and travelled around the tracks with my son John as a sort of glorified mechanic. I was also President of the Birmingham Speedway supporters Club.'

At the time, Tiger said: 'I claim, without hesitation that, with the exception of the maestro Johnnie Hoskins, I have been longer in speedway than any man in England.'

In 1977 the Tiger as made President of the old VSRA, now the World Speedway Riders Association. 'So you see,' he said,'I never really left the bright lights.'

Managing Birmingham in the fifties: Tiger with the 1952 side which he guided to their best First Division performance – they were runners-up to Wembley. From left Ron Mason, Ivor Davies, Tiger, Graham Warren, Bill Jemison. Front, Dan Forsberg, Eric Boothroyd, Alan Hunt and Lionel Watkins.

Star turn: Tiger in his leathers.

Star turn: Tiger out of leathers.

Towards the end of his life the Tiger and I became firm friends and we delighted in sending each other saucy seaside postcards, mainly depicting scantily clad ladies with generous attributes.

I am forever grateful to him, my boyhood hero, for his generous and enthusiastic support of my publication, *Vintage Speedway Magazine*. Without him VSM would never have lasted as long as it did, and possibly certain other now successful nostalgia magazines may never have existed.

Chapter 13

DAYDREAM BELIEVER . . .

THAT small boy looks as if he can't believe his luck that he's managed to get to within touching distance of his speedway hero.

The daydream is, of course, that some day in the cinder-strewn future he'll be putting on a suit of dimpled leathers like that, climbing aboard a magnificent high-powered machine like that and be hearing the cheering crowds shouting his own name.

Maybe that star-struck young chap eventually realised his dream, maybe he didn't, but the man who seems blissfully unaware he is the subject of such singular idolatry certainly did – though not without a struggle.

The dark good looks with the pencil-slim matinee idol moustache belong to Dick Geary. Speedway ran in the family. His father Len rode and his brothers-in-law were the Brine brothers, Wimbledon star Cyril, Ted who managed Wimbledon and Percy, who rode for nine cubs including Glasgow and Rayleigh.

But Dick didn't follow in their wheeltracks immediately. He started earning a crust as a talented commercial artist before turning those talents to the art of cinder shifting, first at Smallford in 1936 and then at West Ham.

After RAF war service as a wireless operator he hung around the Custom House pits again hoping for rides, but that big National League (Division 1) break never came. So he linked up with Sheffield, astonishing a 10,000 crowd and a host of established Northern League (Division 2) stars by winning the Norwich qualifying round of the British Riders Championship.

From then he went on to become a real quality performer for Wigan, Walthamstow and Fleetwood until a series of arm injuries forced him to call quits on his racing career.

Chapter 14
THE 'RED HOT REXTON' RACING SENSATION

YOU won't have heard of Jimmy Rexton. 'Red Hot' Jimmy Rexton, the World Champion speedway rider.

You won't have heard of him because he doesn't exist. At least, not outside the pages of the once hugely popular *Boys' Own Paper* called *The Wizard*. 'Red Hot' Jimmy Rexton rose from unknown junior grass tracker to become the star of the Brixton speedway team and the nation's, as well as the world's, top rider.

All in one single, sensational season.

His story is fiction, of course, but fascinating nonetheless, because anything was possible in *The Wizard* comic.

Among *The Wizard's* other notables was a mysterious athlete who went by the name of Wilson. That's all . . . just Wilson. He dressed in an old one-piece black jump suit, seemed to live in a cave in the remote Border country and, on a diet of raw dandelions, left every other athlete in any Olympic discipline you care to name chasing his shadow. It was hinted that he was some hundreds of years old and, by the way, he always ran barefoot.

There was also – one of my favourites – Nick Smith, a soccer star who played, if memory serves me right, for Barchester United. Or it could have been Tadcaster Rovers. He was the leading light in a tale called *It's Goals That Count* and his team partner on the pitch was an ex-iron puddler named Arnold Tabbs, probably the finest half-back in the Football League. Division One, of course. This was naturally before The Premiership was invented. When the football season ended, Nick strapped on his pads and went out as opening bat in a story called *It's Runs That Count*. A bit of an all-rounder was Nick.

Here are the men who duel with death on the dirt-track
—AND DEATH SOMETIMES WINS!

THE CROWD ROARS FOR REXTON

white line. His action was easy and controlled. Not even when Barnet eased slightly ahead of Spud Charrington did Jimmy worry. After the next bend Jimmy would open up. Wheel to wheel with the other Hartford rider, Jimmy Rexton tore up the straight. Almost into the bend the young Brixton rider shut throttle slightly, and put his machine over to take a sharp turn.

Suddenly a shower of cinders battered against his leathers, stinging his cheekbones and plucking at the crimson silk square bound round his nose and mouth. Blinded temporarily, Jimmy automatically shut right down, and swerved crazily halfway across the track before he could get his machine under control. Clear of the dust cloud and able to see again, Jimmy realised in a flash what had happened, and his bike leaped forward as he twisted the throttle wide open.

The Hartford rider had deliberately thrown away his own chances! In order to stop Rexton he had broadsided deeply, a trick Jimmy was familiar with. Practised a few times, it was quite an easy matter to dig the rear wheel into the track in a sideways fashion, at the same time shutting off and sliding over unhurt, with the bike still in control.

Speeding away along the straight, well behind

Or maybe that was in *The Adventure* comic . . . or perhaps it was in *The Hotspur*. Or even *The Champion*. For sub-teenaged schoolboys seeking an escape from homework, their weekly threepenn'orth was a cornucopia of thrills, excitement and heroism.

The Champion had a fabulous boxing character named Rockfist Rogan of the RAF who, when not knocking out opponents in the fight ring, was knocking out Luftwaffe raiders from the sky.

And I think it was *The Adventure* which had a daring schoolboy pilot who kept his Hurricane hidden in a forest and would emerge periodically to help win the Battle of Britain, and then mysteriously disappear again back to his secret lair among the trees.

But the saga that really held me spellbound was the rise and rise of Red Hot Jimmy Rexton titled *The Crowd Roars For Rexton*. He was called Red Hot Rexton because he rode a crimson bike.

The truth is that speedway has been ill-served by fiction. Before the war there was an obscure epic called *The Missing Speed Ace,* written by Leonard Gribble – a name to conjure with.

One of the most entertaining correspondents to *Vintage Speedway Magazine*, former Newcastle star the late Ivan Crozier, once sent me, as Editor, a splendidly written full length novel full of atmosphere, not only because it was technically accurate, as you would expect, but the story was well crafted, the characters skilfully drawn and the plot well defined.

It never made it to the bookstands because, at the time, it was judged that there was no market for speedway fiction.

Is there now?

The inimitable Dave Lanning, a highly skilled journalist and probably speedway's finest television commentator, has recently published his *Cinderfellas*, a rip-roaring novel set in the 1930s, a time when 'speedway was rock 'n' roll'.

Former promoter and England manager the late John Berry's novel, *Sliding Into Hell*, published by Tony Macdonald's *Retro Speedway* organisation was, according to Macdonald, 'a speculative punt' about which there were 'fairly low sales expectations'.

He went on to report: 'It's fair to say that we were not displeased with the result. Although JB was disappointed it didn't sell as many as he believed it should have done. We have no plans to publish any more fictional tales.'

But the appropriately named Speedway Fiction, a budget imprint, most certainly has, with four speedway themed novels already on offer and a fifth in preparation. Run by

Paul McHarry, a physics teacher turned publisher, he says: 'We have a small but growing customer base – the bulk of which is in Britain, but we post as far afield as Germany. The stories are all set in the 1970s when, as our website claims, Britain was the centre of the speedway world. There is so much more to write about than there would be if the plots were set in the present day.

'My introduction to speedway was in 1969 at Shielfield Park: Berwick v Nelson Admirals – a match I still remember very well. So, it could be said that the 1970s were my formative years in the sport and are therefore the most memorable and the most vivid. Certainly they provided the speedway I recall with the greatest fondness.'

Maybe it is from a fondly remembered youth, but as far as I am concerned the most memorable fictional pure speedway story is about Red Hot Jimmy Rexton.

It starts with Bill Brady, the veteran captain of the newly promoted Brixton speedway team, scouting the local grass track scene for a 'super motorbike rider' to lift his side into being championship contenders.

He spots his man, 'a tall, slim, good looking youth of about twenty-one with slicked back black hair'. He had 'seldom seen a young man in such a fine condition.' Rexton.

Brady knows he's found his man by putting Jimmy through a series of 'accidental' tests, including deliberately dropping his cigarette case – which Rexton catches before it reaches the ground – and causing the scoreboard to totter. Rexton leaps clear just in time.

From Jimmy's reactions, and the fact that he goes out and wins the meeting, Brady is convinced that, 'given another twelve months experience, there wouldn't be a rider in the country to touch Rexton.'

In the dressing tent Brady introduces himself. He says: 'I'm Bill Brady. I've been a bit of a nuisance, but it's been for a purpose.' Rexton rose slowly: 'Not Brady the Brixton speedway captain?' Brady nodded: 'I'd like you to do a cinders trial.' Later Brady learns that Rexton can strip and reassemble an engine by touch alone, and replace one in two minutes.

At the trial Rexton is introduced to his team mates: George Tayler, Les Francis, 'Spud' Charrington, Bert Wilcox and 'Bronco' Joe Cass. As Brady finished the introductions Jimmy, in full leathers and heavy riding boots, 'standing only thirty inches from the five foot high steel fence, bent his knees slightly then, with a terrific upward spring from his toes, vaulted from his standing position clear over the top of the fence.'

Brady and the team put Rexton through a rigorous training routine, relentlessly crowding him, teaching him how to position himself on the track. As Rexton absorbed all he was being taught, and his obvious talent began to assert itself, his team mates' casual acceptance of him 'gradually changed to respect . . . and they began to realize that Rexton was no ordinary rider, and Brady was thinking that here at last was a rider who could be made into the best in the world.'

Rexton made his debut in an away match against Tesford Lions. 'Bewildered and rather overawed, in the pits for the first time in his life, Rexton heard the roar of the crowd like some great wave crashing about his ears.'

Out in the first heat with his captain, it is not quite a storybook debut. Brady, brilliantly team rides Rexton for almost the entire four laps until, with the chequered flag within yards, the Brixton captain roars past his pupil to cross the line first. But with Rexton a safe second, it's a 5 – 1 heat win and Rexton is 'on his way to the hearts of the Brixton fans.'

Before the next practice session Brady enters the team workshops where, unaware of

The Semi-Finals of the British Speedway Riders' Championship!
All the thrills are in this great story.

THE CROWD ROARS FOR REXTON

his presence, Rexton is assembling a speedway machine. Brady watches in astonishment Rexton clamps a two-foot-six-inch by two-inch square length of steel in a vice and bends it at right angles with his bare hands.

'It's a pity your new bike isn't ready,' says Brady. 'You could have tried it out. We start practising in about three quarters of an hour.'

'Give me ten more minutes,' says Rexton, 'I'll have this bike finished.'

When it is wheeled out onto the track 'Brady looked the machine over. It seemed impossible. Yet there it stood, a new bike, completely assembled and without a fault . . . "You've done this in twenty minutes?" he asked slowly.'

The story relates that from then onwards Jimmy Rexton's progress was rapid. The Brixton team and Jimmy start winning a lot, and headlines appear in the local papers: *'New Rider Smashes Track Record'*, above a story that begins: 'Unbeaten in his five races at Brixton Stadium last night, Jimmy Rexton, a rider only just out of the novice stage, made a name for himself by breaking the four lap track record . . . a second faster than that set up by his captain last season.'

Boosted by Rexton, Brixton's continued run of success puts them in a position where they need only one more win to become certain league champions. And Brady tells his star rider he is being dropped from the team . . . 'he had purposely dropped Jimmy so that he didn't form too high an opinion of himself.'

After a moment of stunned silence, Rexton's reaction is: 'Whatever you say, Bill, you're the skipper.' Then, turning aside, he walks quickly away . . . near to tears.

Half way through the meeting Brixton are losing and Brady is desperate. Jimmy's best friend in the team, Spud Charrington, sensing the crisis, fakes a mechanical problem and an injury. So Jimmy is back in and, as his crimson bike is rolled onto the track there is a huge roar from the packed stands as the crowd recognize Rexton.

A couple of rides later and Brixton not only win the match but they are crowned league champions . . . thanks to brilliant riding by Rexton and Brady. 'In the dressing room Brady was unstinting in his praise: "You took chances nobody else would, Jimmy." From outside came a long burst of cheering. "That's because of you – you've put them top of the league," he said. "From next week, you'll have to ride in earnest. I've entered you for the British Riders Championship." '

Rexton is set to come up against the really hard men of the track, 'men who will try every dirty trick in the game.' He witnesses an unpleasant incident involving the Old Cross captain Wizard Firminger who deliberately injures his own team mate, and afterwards Spud Charrington notices a cold and ruthless expression appear on Rexton's face.

In the next Championship meeting Les Francis is killed in a track crash involving a rider named Barnet of the Hartford team, and the two experiences bring about a change in Rexton's attitude to racing. 'Brady knew that Rexton shrank from the unfair tactics and dirty riding that he was encountering, but Jimmy goes out to get Barnet and does so, causing him to crash and break a collar bone.

Now Rexton begins taking chances that endanger not only his own life but the lives of other riders. Bill Brady has no illusions about the state of Jimmy Rexton's mind. It is obvious that he just doesn't care any more. As his captain Brady stages a confrontation. 'Look here, Jimmy,' he says, 'the way you're riding now you'll get yourself killed. We all feel the same way about Les. In speedway these things happen. It only needs one little mistake. Put the affair out of your mind.'

But as Rexton continues his aggressive tactics, Brady tells him: 'You're a selfish fool. If you carry on riding as you are someone is going to get hurt. You can get your points without taking chances.' To which Rexton replies: 'I'll get the points my way.'

The two men have to meet in the last qualifying race that will take them to the final at Wembley and, Rexton realises, Brady has to be beaten like the rest. It comes to the last bend, with Brady leading and Rexton desperately looking for a gap that is not there. But he forces his way through . . . and Brady goes down. Rexton is on his way to the final, but Brady is on his way to hospital with what appeares to be a broken leg.

Rexton watches as the older man is stretchered towards the ambulance. And Brady can see what the shock of what happened has done to Jimmy Rexton. He is once more the young man who he had first signed for Brixton. As Brady is loaded into the vehicle he says: 'Don't feel cut up about it – these things happen. You're the last man in now for Brixton. You're in the final . . . and you can win.'

On the eve of the final, Rexton goes to see Brady in hospital. As he had left the room on a previous visit he was passed by a woman going in. Now Brady says: 'I wasn't aware that you knew Les Francis's mother.' The woman had told him that since Les had been killed, Rexton had insisted she should accept all his prize money.

After discussing tactics for the following day's big final Jimmy Rexton goes home, but he would have been astonished to see the Brixton captain swing both legs out of bed, put on his slippers and walk across the room. His broken leg is a fake.

The final began in driving rain and, on a deteriorating track, Rexton won his first three races but knew he wasn't riding well. 'He had lost his fineness of touch.'

A wheel-to-wheel battle with a northern rider, Tiger Harris, brought a fourth win but they had clashed during the race and it resulted in an injury to Rexton's right leg and right hand.

Before his last ride, Rexton goes to the dressing room and changes out of his sodden leathers into a dry set. Back in the pits he sees a man tinkering with his machine. It is Brady. 'Don't look at me like that,' says Brady. 'I'm afraid I've been pulling your leg. Now you can pull mine as hard as you like, it's not broken.'

He's come, he says, to see Rexton win the championship. 'I put the other engine in your bike myself while you were changing. It's about the finest job of tuning I've ever done.' 'That's good enough for me,' says Jimmy. Brady tells him: 'You are going out there to win the championship. Be as tough as you like, in fact you'll have to be, but get out there and win!'

'Pain shot through Rexton's leg as the riders went into the first bend. His injured hand twisted the throttle fully open. It was to stay that way for the whole of that race and from then on no one in that crowded stadium was seated.

'Vaguely Jimmy saw the chequered flag, and almost fainting with pain, he shut the throttle and saw Brady and the Brixton riders rushing out to congratulate him. It was only when he was standing in the floodlights in front of the Royal Box and some important person has handing him a huge glittering trophy, that he really came to fully realize he had won.

'Jimmy Rexton placed the cup in the hands of the startled Bill Brady. Then he stepped back. The new British Riders Individual Champion was paying tribute to the man who had made him what he was at that minute.'

Extracts from The Crowd Roars For Rexton *by kind permission of D. C. Thomson & Co Ltd.*
The Crowd Roars For Rexton ®© *DC Thomson & Co. Ltd. 2013.*
The author of the Rexton story was Leslie Bell and the artist was Sam Fair.

They're off! Four riders fight for the lead in the race to decide who will be King of the Cinders.

THE CROWD ROARS FOR REXTON

The Road To Wembley

THE big Chevrolet rolled along the country road behind two charabancs which carried supporters of the Brixton Speedway team. Bronco Joe Cass, who drove the car, was talking to Jimmy Rexton, who sat beside him.
"Three thousand fans must have left since

Time passed. Then a light glowed briefly from a bulb in the wall, and a buzzer sounded.
"Ten minutes to go!" remarked George Tayler. There was silence. Charrington took a paper from his pocket. This was the moment that Brady had told him to wait

The late Bill Ritchie creating his funnies at the drawing board.

VINTAGE ARTWORK

WHEN it comes to artwork we are in a different dimension. Speedway has stimulated the imagination of numerous artists, from the broodingly heavy Grimes drawings in the pre-war *Speedway News* magazines and the wonderful Wills cigarette card series of the Thirties, to the mischievous Speedway Sam, the futuristic Streak Storm and the glamorous Zena Lamb in *Speedway Gazette* of the Fifties.

Some of the finest caricaturing was by an artist called Dux in *Speedway Echo* magazine who combined fine artwork with witty comments, again in the Fifties. I recently tried to track him down, but his identity remains a mystery.

The Carver cartoons that appeared in the early post-war Birmingham programmes were simple and elegant. Probably some of the best and most amusing came from the late Bill Ritchie whose cheeky drawings were a regular feature of the *Vintage Speedway Magazine* for years.

But then Bill had the right background, he was one of the artists who contributed to the D.C. Thomson comics, which included such much loved characters as Desperate Dan in the *Dandy* and the *Beano's* Lord Snooty And His Pals, which delighted children for decades.

A dramatic scene from Tiger Annual *1957.*

Opposite, clockwise from top left:

Action from Tiger Annual *1976.*

A 'thrilling incident' as seen by The Tip Top Book *1951.*

The wittily accurate Dux caricature of the Bristol team in Speedway Echo.

A 1947 issue of The Champion *comic featuring speedway and boxing fighter pilot hero Rockfist Rogan of the RAF.*

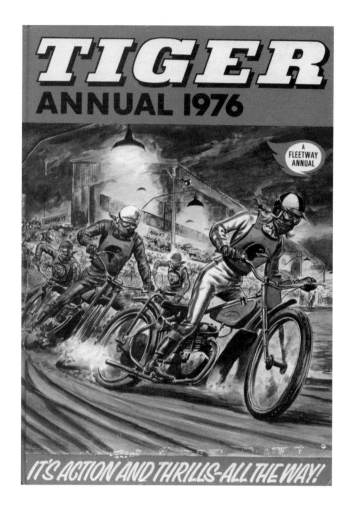

SPEEDWAY SAM

ALL THAT GLITTERS—

Above: *A typical Speedway Sam strip from* Speedway Gazette.

Right: *From Bill Ritchie's Round The Bend series for* Vintage Speedway Magazine.

Far right: *Speedway's fantasy glamour girl Zena Lamb.*

Below: *The futuristic* Speedway Gazette *Streak Storm strip of more than sixty years ago, in which the hero took speedway to the planets racing on bikes that have an uncanny design approaching that of modern closed-in machines.*

STREAK STORM
By DOBSON BROADHEAD

Streak Storm, unbeaten champion of Earth's speedways, is looking for new rivals on other planets. In a space ship invented by his jealous speedway rival, Dyall Rodney, Storm flies into space with Rodney and Streak's sweetheart, Sybil Dean. The space ship crashes on Ash, unknown previously to Earth, and the three adventurers discover that Ash's inhabitants have their own speedways. A race is arranged between Earth and Ash. Rodney tries unsuccessfully to damage Streak's bike before the race.

Chapter 15
SAINT SPLIT

SPEEDWAY'S ORIGINAL LOOSE CANNON WITH A WICKED TWINKLE

SPLIT WATERMAN touched speedway racing with colour and glamour. His escapades – some of the more infamous were light years away from the more conventional letter of the law that the majority of us choose to live by – created blazing headlines. His entire existence has seemed at worst a challenge, at best a monumental laugh. For Split Waterman life has always been for living, and Split Waterman has lived more than most.

And had there not been a Split Waterman someone would have had to invent him.

The honed and athletic physique that, not once but twice, took him to within touching distance of the very pinnacle of the speedway world is much more rounded now. And the matinee idol good looks that set a million female hearts aflutter, on and off the terraces during the great boom years of the sport, when he was lionised – literally – may have faded somewhat over time.

And at ninety, Split still likes the ladies, though.

The thick, jet black curls have turned silver – even the trademark moustache. He has a little difficulty walking distances now – the legacy of war wounds. And a crash at Bradford, almost on the very eve of the 1952 World Championship Final, ruined a kneecap so severely that his wife Avril forcibly had to deny permission to surgeons who wanted to amputate his entire leg.

Such a drastic action would, of course, have destroyed him. It was not the first time he had faced the prospect of losing a limb. Nor would it be the last.

And nor was it the first time someone was 'looking out' for him. There was the darkest of dark Italian war-torn nights when, under a fearful enemy barrage, he unashamedly prayed for his life. There was also the time his Jerusalem hotel was blown up and 91 people were killed.

But the eternal survivor – who has just entered his ninth decade – is still surviving. He has a small hole in the heart condition which, because of his age, he says he is too old for an operation to fix.

Also still surviving is the wicked twinkle in his eye, and no way is the confrontational, opinionated and controversial demeanour diminished that earned him the reputation of being the stormy petrel of British speedway under the telling headline: *Saint Or Sinner?*

On one occasion picket lines of supporters paraded up and down outside Control Board headquarters in central London bearing placards demanding *'Fair Play'* for their hero, who was about to be hauled before the speedway Establishment to explain yet another transgression.

In truth he has been saint *and* sinner. It is a matter of public record that, as well as a dazzling and controversial track career, there has been another career possibly even more colourful and controversial away from the cheering crowds who idolised him.

Though he may have aged proudly, and a touch disgracefully – he would be mortified to be considered boringly conventional – the laugh that launched a thousand quips remains, as unique and impulsive as ever. But that is not the reason, as is popularly supposed, why the entire speedway world who saw his best, and those down the decades who care to recall the star-spangled individualistic personalities like him who shaped the modern sport, know him to this day as just . . . Split.

'I still feel as though I could do it' . . . Split, still laughing at life at ninety.

His full name is Squire Francis Waterman. 'Ha, ha,' he says, 'the new Pope is named Francis. That's my name.'

Squire Francis 'Split' Waterman was twice World No.2, to Jack Young at the infamous 1951 World Final, and to Fred Williams in 1953. He is also the man who finally prised away The Pension, the British Match Race Championship, from the Golden Helmet maestro Jack Parker *(see page 30)*. He was captain of England and the star of teams to the north, south, east and west of British speedway during a career lasting from 1947 to 1962.

In that time he rode for every London club. 'Yes.' he said, 'and every London club I rode for went bust!' The absurdity of the idea, and the memory of it from a distance of more than half a century, triggered again that incredible explosive laugh.

His was a highly turbulent career. He was the archetypal maverick of the sport, the prototype loose cannon.

We are at a table on a balmy evening in Southern Spain beside the marina at Calpe in Alicante with some of his expat friends. He lives a few hundred kilometres down the road and has done for years. It's not easy to get Split Waterman to open up about his swashbuckling speedway days, but once he does . . . well, it's more like he's holding court.

The first thing he did was reveal – exclusively and typically earthily – the real origin of his unique nickname . . . Split. Which we will get to in a moment after we have disposed of the preliminaries, such as that Squire Waterman was born in New Malden, Surrey on 27 July, 1923.

Squaddie Split, somewhere in the Middle East . . . planning his part in Hitler's downfall.

'Bloody, hell, don't keep on. Ninety. Terrible, isn't it?' he says now. When the dreaded day dawns, he says, there won't be a big celebration. 'We might go out to a nice restaurant with friends, that's about all.'

He began to make his way in the adult world as a toolmaker's apprentice. 'I was on ten shillings a week and one shilling and six pence for the union,' he said, 'but I never got the chance to finish it because of the war. I was called up into the forces.' During the conflict he was Mentioned In Despatches.

The obvious and inevitable question was: why were you mentioned in dispatches? Split wouldn't say. He deflected the inquiry by replying: 'That's neither here nor there.' Being Mentioned In Despatches is a military award for gallantry, or otherwise distinguished service, and an official recognition of bravery.

His part in Hitler's downfall took him to, among other places the Middle East, and Italy where, though he wouldn't say in company, he became involved in one of the war's bloodiest and pivotal battles at Monte Casino in 1944. Split vividly revealed in the book *Warzone Speedway*: 'One night, in the darkness, I saw the silhouette of a German paratrooper, and it was very much a case of him or me. I shot him first, but this caused an almighty barrage of gunfire and, while not being a religious man, that night I prayed for my life. I suffered shrapnel wounds to a leg and was sent to an American hospital for treatment. The leg still troubles me on occasions.'

His wounds were so severe that, had he not been able to get swift medical attention, he might well have lost the leg. When he recovered, he was considered unfit for further front-line combat. He said: 'They sent me to 750 BASE Workshops run by a Major William Fearnley *(Major W.W. 'Bill' Fearnley went on to become Manager of the British Speedway Control Board for many years.)* They put up a notice asking for people who could ride motorcycles so I put my name down. We did a 100 mile road race from Naples and I won it – more by luck than judgment – then we started speedway in a running stadium. And I started winning things there.

'They gave me a set of leathers. The leathers were all right but the stitching wasn't very good. I went out on my first day in the leathers and spilt them back to front. They used to call me Split Arse. That's how Split came into it. But of course they couldn't call me Split Arse on the speedway so they just called me Split. That's how the name came about.

'After you'd done so many years with the forces they sent you home on fourteen days leave, and I was overdue for that. So I came back to England and went to see Alec Jackson, the manager at Wembley. *(Split was armed with a letter of introduction from Major Fearnley.)*

Speedway life wasn't all glamour: Split gets help to lift his bike clear of a minor flood.

Alec sent me to Rye House and all I did for the entire fourteen days was go racing at Rye House. Alec signed me up for when I got demobbed and I went back to Italy. They wanted to send me to Japan, but I had sand fly fever, which got me out of trouble. I never went. Then they sent me to Haifa and I was in the King David Hotel in Jerusalem when it was blown up and 91 people were killed – so I was lucky again there.'

When demobilization finally did come Split started to make a name for himself as one of the new wave of up-and-coming young post-war pretenders challenging the big name pioneers who had ruled speedway since the beginning almost twenty years before.

He was keen. A note in the Wembley programme by manager Alec Jackson reported: 'Split Waterman got up at 6.30am Friday morning, the day following the meeting here, to be demobbed from the forces. He hurried back from the demob centre to attend practice here at 11.0am and completed 20 laps before lunch.'

But it was not easy. He had signed for Wembley, an organisation that demanded success

Young man in a hurry: headline-grabber Split challenging the old guard of established veteran pioneers.

The fully-fledged Lion with the all-conquering, all star, 1948 Wembley line-up. From the left: Trainer Tommy Barnett, Bob Wells, Bill Gilbert, George Saunders, Tommy Price (on machine), Fred Williams, Roy Craighead, Wilbur Lamoreaux, Split and manager Alec Jackson.

almost by right, and which also had a very strong team. It was a truly golden era when the sport attracted huge crowds each week, not only to the Empire Stadium but to tracks all over the country. At Wembley they often had bigger attendances than for FA Cup Finals, and it was not unknown for thousands to be locked outside on race nights.

There were on average 75,000-plus customers paying to see speedway at Wembley regularly on Thursday nights. 'Wembley Stadium could pay everyone on the staff from the sale of programmes alone,' said Split. So where did all the rest of the money go? Who had it? 'Well', he said, 'Elvin did *(Sir Arthur Elvin was then virtually the owner of the Empire Stadium)*, or if he didn't he was a fool. And he wasn't a fool. He was the best friend speedway ever had.'

At that time there was world class speedway racing every weekday in London – Wimbledon Mondays, West Ham Tuesdays, New Cross Wednesdays, Wembley Thursdays and, from 1947, Harringay Fridays. On Saturdays the show moved north to Belle Vue Manchester and Odsal Bradford. You also had the choice of buying five or six speedway magazines from any corner news stand on the streets of London.

There was a rider-pooling system designed to even out team strengths when league racing resumed in 1946. Jackson chose only his pre-war Wembley stars Tommy Price and George Wilks plus former Belle Vue international Bill Kitchen. Reporting the make-up of the new teams, *Speedway News* magazine revealed that, apart from the virtually unknown Bob Wells, the remainder of the Wembley team would come 'from the Rye House school'. The 'remainder' were Alf Bottoms, Bill Gilbert, Roy Craighead and Bronco Wilson. No Waterman. And under Jackson's brilliance, Wembley were the first post-war National League (Division 1) champions.

Split was a young man in a hurry, and to get into a championship-winning side he had to hustle. 'You've got to remember, I was pushing my way in,' said Split. 'I mean, I pushed

Bob Wells out because he was reserve.' But in an amazingly short time his flair and his talent won him a permanent place as a Wembley Lion.

'I was in the team after two weeks,' he said. Before 1947 was half way through he was being hailed as 'the find of the season'. He was, said the report, scoring consistently and Alec Jackson told *Speedway News* that, apart from his do-or-die-style brilliant riding, 'Split is invaluable for his high spirits, He keeps the side laughing however the luck goes.'

Only weeks later he really had the speedway world gasping when the headline: *Duggan Beaten By Waterman* appeared. Vic Duggan was in superlative form for Harringay and recognised then as the number one rider in the world. In 1947 he was virtually invincible, so it was big news when Split, who had barely shaken off his brash newcomer image, claimed the scalp of the mighty Australian. It was in Heat 9 of a British Speedway Cup match at Wembley when 'Waterman took a flyer from the gate and led Vic Duggan throughout. The Harringay captain managed to get within a length of Waterman on the second lap but just could not overtake.'

The sensation had *Speedway News* asking: 'What is it that this fellow Split Waterman has that others haven't? In one season he has climbed into the headlines more times than any other known novice. Split certainly has something, and it takes more than a hearty laugh to be able to give Vic Duggan a tousing. He has . . . a fan mail and support equal to a star . . . and whatever he has, there's all the makings of a future star in this young rider. He possesses the instincts of a man who knows where he is going and the quickest way to get there – and, accidents ruled out, he's going to the top'.

The top, however, was still some way away, but by September he *was* a star. He was selected to represent London against the Australians, and nearly all the major world talent, other than Jack and Norman Parker, was in that. For London, Split's Wembley skipper Bill Kitchen was there and so was his Wembley team mate George Wilks, plus West Ham captain Eric Chitty and Jeff Lloyd and Geoff Pymar of New Cross, all full internationals. For Australia there were Vic Duggan, New Cross captain Ron Johnson, former World Champion Lionel Van Praag also of New Cross, Max Grosskreutz of Bradford and Aub Lawson of West Ham. Reserves were Ray Duggan and Frank Dolan of Harringay. Split scored 10 points helping London to win 61 - 47. You could say that he had arrived.

Off the track there were all sorts of Waterman fun and games at Wembley. There was the time he completely destroyed Alec Jackson's new Vauxhaul car, fresh out of the showroom. Alec had taken it to Wembley to show it to his friends. He parked it near the workshops right behind Split's Hudson Terraplane coupe which he was working on at the time. It had no proper seats and Split was perched on a wooden box which slipped. His foot just happened to be on the accelerator and the vehicle was in reverse, causing it to shoot backwards . . . right into Jackson's pride and joy, virtually folding it in two.

'It was brand, spanking new,' said Split. 'I went straight into it and the thing ended up in a V-shape.'

Talk about slapstick.

There were other escapades. Split said: 'I'd been to America, and when I came back I went to Elvin and said I wanted to sell hot dogs in a roll at the stadium, like they do in the States. He said he was very sorry but he couldn't allow me to do that because it was degrading. A couple of years later they were doing it.

'The people who worked at Wembley were ex-Old Bill – the police. And that's how I used to get out of trouble . . . What sort of trouble? You name it, I've done it. I was always in trouble for speeding.'

Within a year Split was a regular in the England team and being nominated as a challenger for the Golden Helmet, the great Jack Parker's British Match Race Championship. In the first Test of the season at Wimbledon, Split's international debut, he scored six points in England's 61 - 45 win, but was damned with faint praise. The match report said: 'The English pairing of Tommy Price and Split Waterman did not come up to expectations although both put everything they had into their riding. Tommy seemed to be weighed down with the responsibility of introducing a newcomer to the Test series . . . and perhaps gave Waterman too many opportunities to demonstrate his sometimes unconventional – but admittedly productive – methods of racing.'

Yet in June, Split confounded his critics by winning the prestigious London Riders Championship at New Cross against formidable opposition – Vic and Ray Duggan, home skipper Ron Johnson, who Split pushed to a new track record in the first race, Tommy Price, Eric Chitty, Aub Lawson and Malcolm Craven of West Ham. He was then described as 'Wembley Lions' wonder man' and it earned him his crack at the Golden Helmet. But

Above left:
The Royal handshake: Prince Phillip is introduced to Split before the Speedway Riders Championship Final at Wembley in 1948. Split finished joint fourth with team mate Bill Gilbert.

Above right:
In the company of the sport's finest: Split's Harringay captain, the great Vic Duggan, hands out some sage advice to the man who was – at the time – speedway's costliest star. Looking on, their team mate Danny Dunton.

he lost the first leg of his challenge and had to pull out of the second because of a leg injury. His time would come.

For champion Parker it all resulted in a painful circumstance. When Split was unable to take part, it was decided to substitute a match between Jack and his Belle Vue team mate Dent Oliver, another newcomer hitting the headlines. A broken chain pierced the Parker leathers, inflicting deep lacerations to his buttocks and he had to be assisted from his machine.

Split went on to win a place in the World Championship substitute, the Speedway Riders Championship Final, finishing fourth in front of 90,000 spectators at Wembley as Vic Duggan took the title.

It is no wonder, then, that the Old Guard in the Lions' den should feel a certain amount of antagonism toward the young upstart who had reached speedway stardom in a fraction of the time it had taken them, and seemingly with little effort. After all, the promising careers they had set out to forge in the Thirties had been frustrated by six years of war. Did the big names, such as Bill Kitchen and Tommy Price resent him?

'Yes,' said Split. 'Bill Kitchen was very crafty. They always reckoned that Kitch was a good team man – which he was. Though there came a time when I knew I could beat him. He would team ride you in and then, right on the line, he would take first place from you. He would never let me win. What I didn't know, but found out later, was that he was on double money.

'We'll, it's not sour grapes or anything, but there were . . . fiddles among the big names at Wembley, which they were entitled to because I did the same at Harringay.

'Some of them had been around since before the war, and you couldn't get into their league. I couldn't get into the money because of Tommy Price and Bill Kitchen. They got their normal start and points money, but they were really on double pay, and they monopolised the second half winnings. You could sometimes earn as much money in the second halves as you could in a match. I learned from that.'

And that was why in 1950 he left Wembley, speedway's most successful and glamorous club, for Harringay. While he had been at Wembley the team had won three league titles, the National Trophy and the London Cup. He was also turning his back on a home track that could easily have been to his advantage in the newly resurrected World Championship. Every Final then was held at the Empire Stadium.

He became the most expensive rider in speedway, going for what was a record transfer fee for the times. 'Harringay wanted me and they paid £3,000,' he said. 'And then I did what Tommy and Bill were doing at Wembley, because I became the top guy at Harringay. And what I got – shall we say – legally I got in cash.'

Around this time, Wimbledon boss Ronnie Greene was promoting Sunday meetings in Ireland at Shelbourne Park in Dublin. Split said: ' Ronnie wouldn't bring all the money back himself, so I used to bring it back – fifteen-sixteen hundred pounds at a time. Customs once took one of my bikes to bits, but that time I didn't have anything in it. Howdy Byford, of West Ham, he used to bring back nylon stockings hidden in the wheels of his bike. We used to take out the inner tubes from the tyres and fill them with stockings. In those days you couldn't buy nylons in England and they went for £3 a pair. I used to make more money selling stockings than I did racing.'

When speedway's costliest star arrived to be part of the Harringay entertainment

Pinching the Pension . . . the reign is over: new title holder Split holds the Golden Helmet while being given a lift by Jack Parker after taking the British Match Race Championship from the old maestro at Harringay in 1951. Jack's leathers tell the story . . .

Jokers wild: Trevor Redmond (left) and Split bring out their bikes for a photoshoot with the leggy showgirls from Wembley's Empire Pool . . . and a bit of mutually beneficial publicity.

complex at Green Lanes in North London, the 'entertainment' didn't stop. There was the famous occasion when Split drove the track steamroller into manager George Kay's office. It was one of those Waterman larks. He knew how to start the thing, but not how to stop it. It did stop in the end, but it had a helpless George watching in horror as the steel leviathan bore down on him, and shouting because he couldn't get out.

Split was now in the company of the sport's finest. The magnificent Vic Duggan was the Harringay captain: how did they get on? 'He was as good as gold,' said Split, 'I rather liked him. He was quite a nice bloke. He didn't resent me.'

But the great Australian's chance of becoming the official World Champion, which at one time had seemed inevitable, was slipping away. Injury had prevented him from qualifying for the 1949 Final and the subsequent death of his brother Ray in a racing accident in Sydney hastened his decision to quit the sport. It left the number one Harringay spot vacant for Split, who then made the first of his five World Final appearances, finishing seventh on eight points.

Eventually there came another crack at Parker's Pension. The career of Jack, the old warhorse, was also on the wane. He had set a magnificent, still unequalled, record of defending the Golden Helmet 21 times against almost all-comers since 1946 – at one time he survived 13 consecutive challenges. Only two men had taken the Match Race crown from him, Duggan and Aub Lawson, and he had always won it back. Age was not on Jack's side – he was then forty-five – but it was on Split's, and Split finally put an end to Parker's reign in 1951.

'I was the one who took it off him in the end,' said Split. 'But as soon as I did the "pension"– £1 a day – was stopped. What used to happen with Parker . . . he was very clever. You could always tell a big motor. On a "small" motor, one within the rules, you would hear a high revving brrrrrrrrrrrrrrr . . . but Parker would go by and you'd hear a boom, boom, boom, slow revving noise, so you knew he was on a "big one".

'Now the ruling in the speedway game was that if you thought there was trouble you had to get hold of a steward as soon as you got back to the pits and tell him to check that bike. What they did was take the top off and check the size. But as soon as Jack came in someone would come and take away the bike he'd ridden. It wasn't his bike, he'd borrowed it, and you couldn't do much about it.'

Such rumours had been round speedway's dark alleys for years, and Parker was certainly aware of them. It was well known that Parker usually rode a rough looking bike owned by team mate Ron Mason in the Golden Helmet series, after theatrically discarding what he called his 'spit and polish' machine. In an interview with me many years ago he said that his show of changing machines before a Match Race was part of his plan to psych out his challengers. He insisted: 'No, the bike wasn't oversized, it conformed to all the rules. And yes, it's true, there were bits of wire apparently holding it together, but I assure you it had no real use – other than to kid my opponent.'

'But I still beat him,' said Split. 'I held the Golden Helmet until I had an accident and they took it away from me.' Split even employed similar tactics to Parker. He said: 'I could demoralise some riders just by going up to the line. I'd say to them: "Do you want to borrow my bike, and I'll take the spare? And it worked. I used to bugger 'em up before they started.'

In the long time tradition of the Golden Helmet, controversy followed it – and Split – around. He and Jack Young were to race for the title and Split surprised everyone by agreeing to the first leg being raced on Young's home track at West Ham. 'Now Jack Young was a nice chap,' said Split. 'We went out for the first race and unfortunately he caught me and arse over tip I went.

'Well, not a problem, have a re-run. Then it was announced that the race had been awarded to Jack Young. Which was wrong, we should have had a re-run. Instead the steward (referee) gave Jack the race. So I did the wrong thing, I stuck

The joust with authority that caused a bit of a riot at West Ham: Split after protesting strongly to the steward (referee) over the Match Race incident with Jack Young. Manager Wal Phillips is in close support.

Saint or Sinner ?

Asks Jim Stenner

1952 was "Split" Waterman's headline year. Repeatedly through the season he was duelling with the Control Board or was it vice versa ?

To get the back-ground go back to August, 1951, when "Split" took the British Match Race title from Jack Parker but, declining to defend fairly quickly, claimed the full six weeks allowance before meeting and beating Aub Lawson.

Later the "holding" period was lessened to four weeks, the third paragraph, reg. 572, being amended to :

" The Winner shall hold the title for not less than four weeks. If, however, in consequence of injuries it appears to the Board unlikely that the Holder will be able to defend his title within four weeks of the conclusion of the previous competition, then the Board shall declare the title void and shall nominate two other riders to compete . . ."

In May, 1952, Waterman, unable through injury to fulfil v. Ronnie Moore on May 26th and 30th (one month after his April 22nd and 25th tussle with Jack Young), was relieved of the title under the rule quoted.

Waterman who needed only another week thought the application harsh. So did Harringay, whose protest against the forfeiture was rejected by the Board's Appeals committee.

In June, Waterman, selected to tackle Young, came down first time round at West Ham as Jack dived through on the inside. For safety reasons the race was stopped.

"Waterman will be fit for the re-run" blared the 'speakers as he returned to the pits. Both men started from the same positions and "Split," from the outside, won by 10-15 lengths.

Reaching the pits he was informed that the first race had been awarded to Young by the steward making it 1-1. The next run, therefore, would be the decider. "Split" protested strongly to the steward and withdrew.

At a subsequent Control Board inquiry Waterman was severely reprimanded. Official statement : "A Court appointed by the Speedway Control Board to-day

Waterman, leaving the 'phone booth in West Ham's pits after protesting strongly to the steward. Beside him, Harringay team manager Wal Phillips.

9

Fair Play for their hero: Split's Fans demonstrate outside the Control Board offices in central London as he attends the disciplinary hearing over the Match Race walkout at West Ham – it earned him a severe reprimand.

my fingers up, didn't I? And walked off. That caused a bit of a riot, I'm afraid. I had to have a police escort out of the place. Shouldn't have done that. But I was like that . . . you know what I was like.'

When he was summoned before the authorities to explain his actions, it led to a demonstration in Pall Mall outside the Control Board offices with fans carrying placards demanding *'Fair Play For Split Waterman'*. Split said: 'They called Jack and I to an inquiry and decided that the steward was wrong. They wanted to re-stage it all, but I didn't want to do it.'

It was at this point in his career that he came closest to being World Champion in the drama-soaked 1951 World Final. It was dramatic for three reasons: Split Waterman came within a whisker of being crowned champion of the world, Australia's Jack Young became the first Second Division rider to win the title, and his fellow countryman, Jack Biggs, came within one single point of glory . . . and fluffed it. Twice.

The climax came in Heat 19 – well, it proved to be more of an anti-climax really. Biggs, Split's team mate at Harringay, had ridden to four straight wins. He was on 12 points. Jack Young was also on 12, but had completed his rides. So Biggs needed a single point from his last outing to take the World Championship. His opponents were Fred Williams, Aub Lawson and . . . Split Waterman, who needed to win to force a run-off with Young for a rostrum place.

As the riders prepared to go out for the vital race, in the pits Aub Lawson approached Fred Williams and said: 'Has Jackie said anything to you?' Fred said he hadn't. The truth was that Jack Biggs was convinced the title was his. He was so confident – arrogant was the word used years later when this incident was extensively analysed – that he could win he had no need to ask the others to 'stay out of his way,' as was conventional practice and quite expected in such circumstances.

Split said: 'By winning the World Championship you earned good money, but I always said I'd never give any money for points in a championship.'

When the four riders left the tapes in Heat 19, Biggs was crowded out on the first bend and finished last. The incident that took place on that controversial first turn has been discussed and dissected ever since. (*Jack Biggs's widow Sheila revealed exactly what did happen in our previous volume* Speedway Superheroes.) But at the chequered flag Split was first, Lawson was second, Williams was third and Biggs was last. The result put Split into a run-off with Young for the title and gave Biggs a second chance, with all of them on 12 points.

*It doesn't get much
friendlier than this . . .
rival Test captains
holding hands: Split
and Ronnie Moore
strike a slyly amused
pose for the camera.
Behind Ronnie Moore,
Graham Warren
wonders what to
make of it all.*

'When it came to the race,' said Split, 'I changed my bike and Jackie Biggs managed to get in front of me. The only thing I can say about that race is that Jack Biggs was going to block me in all ways because Youngie won the race. By the time I got by him it was too late. Jack Young was too far in front.'

It was a cataclysmic result, what with Biggs failing – twice – and Young, then with Second Division Edinburgh, taking the title under the noses of all the big international First Division stars.

The following season came the accident at Bradford. Split said: 'I hurt my knee and knocked out two front teeth. When I went to hospital there was an argument between the two surgeons. They were going to take my leg off. So Avril got on to Wally Phillips, who was the manager at Harringay at the time. They were only going to chop my leg off, and the argument was about who was going to do the operation.

'The knee was so bad apparently that they thought amputation was the best thing to do.'

Avril said: 'I had a row and told them I was not moving out of the ward, and Wally came up straight away and we took Split out.'

'They took me back to the Royal Northern.' said Split, 'where they were using a serum on footballers. They injected it into my knee and put a new cap in . . . and I qualified for the World Final at Wembley, and rode. There was some suggestion that the doctors would not allow me to race, but I did a few runs and it was all right – it hurt, mind you.' The injury was too much of a handicap, and Split finished twelfth on six points. It was another near miss the following season: second again to Fred Williams. There was a last World Final in 1954 and a fifth place.

He made more than thirty appearances for England and, during his time at Harringay, Split led the Racers to the National Trophy and the Coronation Cup. But the club was one of the first top outfits to feel the chill wind of the oncoming speedway recession and the doors were closed after the 1954 season. Split was directed to Belle Vue . . . and refused to go *(though 19 points are recorded against his name for the Aces in 1962)*.

'I just didn't want to go there,' he said. 'You've got to remember that at the time I was running a plastics factory. I used to make the Airfix stuff, model aeroplanes and all that. I was also making household goods. With a twelve inch bowl you had to pay VAT, but if I made it at eleven-and-a-half inches you didn't. I was up to all the dodges.

'But I got into trouble with one – that was the gold. I had made the tool for a £20 gold piece and they found it. It's now in the museum at the Bank of England. Still there. At that time you were getting £80 for them. It took me about two months to make it, and do you know, I never used it – never used it. But it was a laugh, though.'

Not such a laugh was the accident he had in the plastics factory. 'I slipped and the

*Opposite page
Top: One for all and
all for Harringay,
but it was every man
for himself at the
1950 World Final:
Danny Dunton
(left), Split and Vic
Duggan.*

*Bottom: Second
again. Two years
after finishing
runner-up to World
Champion Jack
Young in 1951, a
repeat performance
for Split behind Fred
Williams (centre).
Third man is Geoff
Mardon.*

The smooth and the spectacular. Old rivals Jack Young and Split – a confrontation guaranteed to bring in the crowds.

machinery severed a finger,' said Split. 'I wrapped it up in a hanky, put it in my pocket and took it to hospital. There I was told to wait while they went through: what's your name, and all that. I said: "Wait a minute, I haven't got a finger. It's in my pocket." Well, they got me a little nurse and she undoes the hanky – and faints. Fell on the floor. Then in comes one of the surgeons who thinks I've been playing around . . . that's how daft it got.

'Anyway, they sewed the finger back on, stitched it up and sent me home the next day. But the finger used to stick out, which was awkward. So I went back and they took a leader out of my thumb and put it in my finger. Each finger has two leaders, so now when I hurt my finger I hurt my thumb, and when I hurt my thumb I hurt my finger. Ha, ha!'

Are you still with us . . .?

With the closure of Harringay Split did the rounds: West Ham, Southampton, New Cross, a brief spell back at Wembley, Ipswich and Wimbledon, where he had a monumental bust-up with promoter Ronnie Greene. 'I forget what it was about,' said Split. It was about objecting to being pulled out of a ride.

'I went into the showers to change and he came rushing in and ordered me out. I told him I wouldn't go. So he went out and made an announcement to the crowd that he would never have Split Waterman racing on his track again – something like that.'

The trouble was that there was probably more going on in Split's life off the track than on, and he was then in the twilight of his career. He finally called it a day in 1962. 'After my last race at Ipswich I was never paid,' he said. 'I just walked out. I was never paid at all. There were a lot of them doing that, you know.'

It was a long career. So what was the outstanding moment?

'Dunno,' he said. 'Parker. The Golden Helmet. It was nice to get it away from him. Two seconds in the World Championshp. I was quite happy with what I did. I often regret, in a way, that I left Wembley, because of Wembley's name. I mean Harringay was a good name but, in my opinion, it was just another stadium on the other side of Town. There was a magic about Wembley.

'It's difficult to pick an outstanding moment. I just liked racing. What I liked more than anything was winning. But I liked the challenge. I never believed in practising. I never went to practises before World Finals. I wanted a racing situation. You have to be hungry, like a boxer.'

He commutes regularly between his home in southern Spain and England on business trips. Has done for years. 'Just travelling around, you know what I'm like. Just to see people I know.'

It is a long time now since he was actively involved in speedway, half a century. Are there any regrets?

'Only that I'd like to be still doing speedway, but that's out of the question, isn't it? Will I be watching the Grands Prix on television this season – of course. What do I think of it? Well they have it all, don't they? Bikes, mechanics all over the place. I'm a little bit jealous, in a funny sort of way. Know what I mean? They're making a fortune. I think they can make more in one meeting than I did in a year.

'But when I watch it on television I see things, you know, all this business at the gate. A lot of old cobblers that is. And they are fast, but they know only one thing – on or off. They go round the outside and they don't seem to be in control a lot of the time. It looks like hard work.

'I still feel as though I could do it. I'd like to have another try at it. I'd like to have a go. Maybe have a ride when there's nobody watching. Speedway . . . I know it's only a sport, but in the beginning – right at the beginning – I'd have raced for nothing. Just for the thrill of it.

'Till I realised the money . . .'

THE OTHER HEADLINES . . .

SPLIT made lurid headlines in the late 1960s away from speedway. His involvement is a matter of public record.

In 1967 he was arrested at Newhaven while attempting to board a ferry to Dieppe after gold with a value of £10,000 was found in the chassis of his fiancée Avril Priston's car.

A subsequent raid at Priston's family home in Bedfordshire found illegal firearms. Waterman was convicted in 1968 of attempting to smuggle gold out of Britain, as well as unlawful possession of firearms including two sub-machine guns, two rifles, and three pistols, and possession of dies for forging coins. He was sentenced to four years in prison. The gold was thought to have come from a bullion van robbery in Clerkenwell.

Priston was convicted of conspiracy to smuggle gold and possession of two pistols and a pen gun, and was sentenced to six months in prison.

In his book *Nipper Read: The Man Who Nicked The Krays,* Leonard 'Nipper' Read of the Metropolitan Police, who was part of the team which brought the Great Train Robbers to justice, described Split as 'the flamboyant former speedway star' and 'one of the sport's glamour boys.'

Read was trying to find evidence of a conspiracy to kill a man using a trick suitcase. He recounted a meeting with Split who he said was 'ingenious, producing a truly deadly murder weapon'. Split, he claimed, was a friend of an accomplice of the infamous London gangsters the Kray twins. Read went on: 'Waterman was then serving a prison sentence for gold smuggling. He agreed he had made a suitcase of which he was rather proud, calling it "a beautiful piece of craftsmanship" – but was unable to say anything else.'

'It *was* a beautiful piece of craftsmanship. It was designed to allow a syringe to be hidden in the fabric with a needle protruding through the outer hide of the case. By pulling a small ring near the handle the content of the syringe could be discharged. Waterman realized, of course, it was to be used to kill someone but he had neither the name of the proposed victim nor who was to use it.

'Indeed he made the point that one of his conditions when he made the case was that he was not to be told such details.

'When the Home Office pathologist examined the case he described it as the most deadly weapon he had ever seen. He said that had it been used properly the victim would have been dead within eight seconds. He also added that the effect of the proposed poison would be to simulate a heart attack and no one would be able to identify it as murder with the sole exception of himself.'

Split and Avril married in 1970 at Caxton Hall, London. They live in Nerja on Spain's Costa del Sol.

Chapter 16

THE SECRET LIFE OF BASIL STOREY

I MAKE no apology for this. It is by way of homage to someone I have admired for approximately three score years and ten . . . a lifetime in anyone's sense let alone the biblical.

He was a true artist of the track . . . though he never to my knowledge ever wore a set of leathers, never so much as sat on a speedway bike or, in consequence, never felt the need to put on a crash helmet. Yet he was a speedway genius.

I know for a fact that he never travelled faster than a London double-decker bus, yet he rode to fame amassing – and losing – a transient fortune on . . . a typewriter. He was a maestro of the speedway prints.

In the annals of sporting journalism he may not have reached the eminence of the Daily Mail's award-winning Ian Wooldridge, cricket's E.W. Swanton of the Telegraph, boxing's Peter Wilson of the Mirror, golf's Peter Salliss of the BBC, Formula One's Murray Walker or that great broadcasting all-rounder David Coleman.

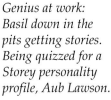

Genius at work: Basil down in the pits getting stories. Being quizzed for a Storey personality profile, Aub Lawson.

He was never credited with an immortal sporting phrase such as 'They think it's all over . . . it is now,' with which Kenneth Wolstenholme wrapped up England's finest soccer hour in 1966.

But when it came to speedway racing he was definitely in the Ivan Mauger, Tony Rickardsson, Ove Fundin and Barry Briggs class.

He was Basil Storey. I write about him in the past tense because he has been dead these

thirty-nine years. I know what his final mortal words were, but I shall save them till last because they are the most apt and uproarious journalistic payoff imaginable. That's according to his widow Rene who, when she revealed them to me, expressed her hope that her dear, departed husband knows what they were because he would think them hilarious.

And why wouldn't I be honouring his memory with such magnanimity? Because, my friends, Basil Storey had the great good sense and fine editorial judgment to commit to print the very first words I wrote about speedway all of . . . oh, sixty-five years ago now. The revelation of which – like his final words – will come later. For the present it is sufficient for you to know that if it hadn't been for dear old Two Gun Baz, as he fondly called himself, you wouldn't be reading this now.

He died not far from where he was born, at Low Fell, County Durham, just off the famous Road To Blaydon Races. Maybe that well known and roistering song of the north country common man setting out to enjoy himself had something to do with the way Basil Storey communicated to the common fan, passing through the one-shilling-and-thrupenny turnstiles, at speedway tracks all over the country, all the romance, the drama, the excitement, the absurdity and the glory that is speedway racing.

He grafted at it, beginning as a junior reporter on the *Newcastle Chronicle*. 'It was a magnificent grounding,' he said. 'For thirty shillings (£1.50p) a week I often worked eighteen hours a day, seven days a week. In those days you didn't specialize. You had to have a knowledge of every sport.'

In this pursuit he covered the entire sporting spectrum, including football, horse racing and speedway, writing under the name of Clutch Start, and even staging boxing shows for charity. Five years as an infantryman during the war finally formed the inbred grit and no-nonsense Geordie that was Basil Storey's uncompromising journalistic character.

Back in The Print he had been drawn to London and the Fleet Street village where he became one of the editorial team of two on *Speedway Gazette,* which was launched, price 3d (1.5p), upon an eager and enthusiastic public on 15 April, 1946 from No.180 on that famous boulevard of ink . . . or Street Of Shame, depending on your point of view.

Well, actually, during the winter *Speedway Gazette* became *Ice Hockey & Speedway Gazette,* and every Easter it miraculously transformed itself back to *Speedway Gazette* once more.

It was a pathetic little publication to begin with. For one thing there was paper rationing in 1946, which kept it down to a meager eight pages. For another it appeared to be run by only Basil and Tom Morgan, who was also *Broadsider* of *The People* Sunday newspaper.

At first there were no bylines. The main story on the front page was always *By The Editor,* but as it got into its stride the Storey name suddenly appeared on page one. Then, to disguise the lack of staff Basil also gave himself the names of William B. Whitley, Charlie Lamb and Will Shakespeare – only the best for Basil.

In addition to his *Gazette* duties he was editing two boys' magazines, was soccer, speedway and ice hockey reporter for the *Daily Express* and working for the racing paper *Sporting Record* at the same time. Any spare moments he had were taken up in writing Dixon Hawk detective stories, science fiction and adventure tales for *Boys' Own Paper*-style publications, even though, Rene revealed, he disliked children intensely.

Whatever, the man's application was phenomenal. Rene said: 'Five nights a week between April and November we went to speedway meetings in London. I used to fill in the programmes and keep a scoring record of the meetings, he would be in the pits getting stories. Then he would often stay up all night writing his speedway reports, and in the mornings go off to his office in Fleet Street.'

Basil Storey's industrious nature and the wit, wisdom and sheer entertainment with which he filled his *Speedway Gazette* pushed up the circulation to a peak of 95,000 a week.

By then the magazine was selling (in old money) at 6d (5p) a week, representing an amazing £2,500 – or very near. In today's values, that's an astonishing £60,000 Basil was pulling in weekly for the *Gazette's* owners, a pair of eccentrics by all accounts. Rene said: 'There was money all over the place.'

Basil took on some help, a young man named Harry Carpenter who went on to earn fame as a boxing broadcaster and enjoy a whimsical relationship with Frank *'Know What I Mean Harry'* Bruno. When I once approached (now the late) Mr Carpenter and asked to interview him about his days at the *Gazette,* Mr Carpenter declined to meet me. I suspected

Two Gun Baz, he called himself: The cartoon of Basil which used to appear above his hard-hitting and racy letters pages called Pass The Aspirin.

that was because the by then exalted Mr Carpenter would rather his public knew as little as possible about his previous association with speedway racing.

A pity because what they dished up every week in the *Gazette* was mesmeric. All speedway life was there, from the brightest stars and their big name exploits to the humble and unsung heroes who were lucky if they got a mention once a season.

There were personality features, tales of speedway's rich and historic past, a cycle speedway section, cartoon characters such as superhero Red Rogan, Cinder Sue and Speedway Sam, crossword puzzles, quizzes, a speedway Who's Who, the sport's best gossip column called *Goggles & Gauntlets*, a hard-hitting editorial entitled *Both Sides Of The Safety Fence*, readers' letters, pen pals, special offers, *Junior Gazette* – which is where I came in, and yes I'm coming to that – plus of course reports and a results service which, according to Rene, earned the correspondents the princely sum of two guineas a time.

There was a vein of literary gold running through what Storey did, and in a section of the journalistic trade now frequently populated by scribblers whose cliché-ridden efforts struggle to compose a coherent sentence, it was refreshing to encounter a headline which proclaimed: *Three Speedway Musketeers: One For All And All For Harringay.*

Under it Storey reported: *'Three adventurous Australians, like the three famous Musketeers which Alexander Dumas gave to posterity, have answered the call of their D'Artagnan to sally forth on a new exploit.*

'Harringay chief Fred Whitehead, pre-war Hackney Wick mastermind, sought a team for his north London track, and in much the same manner as Athos, Porthos and Aramis of old flew to the side of their leader, Vic and Ray Duggan and Frank Dolan have dashed from the other side of the world to do battle for Harringay under the Whitehead banner . . .'

Then there was the strange affair of the Haunted Hammers. Readers learned that no one *'had been able to report the unwelcome presence of a poltergeist in the West Ham workshops, and no ghostly speedway ace had been witnessed broadsiding silently round the pits bend as the clocks of East London chimed the witching hour of midnight. But for all that Custom House is haunted.'*

The 'ghost' turned out to be merely ill-luck. A contrived triviality? Maybe. But what atmosphere? What an angle?

And perhaps so was this headline: *Bronco Buster Is Going To Town.* Beneath that was a

Baz's winning team … some of them real, some of them figments of his fertile imagination. Along the back row: John Alexander (real), Robin Richmond (real), William B. Whitley, Harry Packford, Zena Lamb, Dobson Broadhead (real). Front: Speedway Sam, Will Shakespeare, Roy Fellows (real), Eric Chitty (real), Basil (real), Charlie Lamb.

Your Editor asked artist Dobson Broadhead to give his impression of the GAZETTE Editorial Department on Press Day. Above is the result. For your guidance the GAZETTE staff as seen by Broadhead are as follows : *Back row* (left to right): John Alexander, Robin Richmond, William B. Whitley, Harry Packford, Zena Lamb, Dobson Broadhead. *Front row:* Speedway Sam, Will Shakespeare, Roy Fellows, Eric Chitty, Basil Storey and Charlie Lamb. (Story of the cartoon on page 10.)

paragraph or two of this: *'He speaks with the lazy drawl of a cowboy and has the swinging gate of a diminutive Texan . . . His freckled, weatherbeaten features suggest a character from the pages of Zane Grey [a contemporary Western adventure novelist], or maybe he reminds you of one of [cowboy film star] Hopalong Cassidy's buddies. He has a way with horses, that is why his schoolboy pals way home in Australia christened him Buck. Until recently, however, he had little luck with speedway "horses" . . .'*

It was a story in the wonderful *And The Gods Smiled* series, a touching tale about the little Australian Buck Whitby – never a star and an unfashionable rider who was shunted around from track to track – who had saved the day for his team, though pale and ill and more in need of a bed than a speedway saddle.

Basil wrote: *'The speedway Gods gurgled with undisguised glee. The gallant Whitby had gone to the starting gate alongside his skipper Vic Duggan with Harringay needing a 5 – 1 to draw the match against the all conquering Wimbledon side. Buck was in no condition to make a flier, and the speedy Duggan had to almost stop the race to let his partner through. The Dons' Dick Harris fell off in astonishment and his partner George Saunders was unable to break through the Duggan-Whitby combination.'*

Another tantalising triviality? Yes, but also an incident of triumph against the odds. The magic formula.

Basil's editorials were fearless. He was of the opinion that the Golden Helmet British Match Race Championship events were a throwback to speedway's long gone circus sideshow days – and said so, even though his opinion was confounded by the huge crowds who packed the terraces every month to see the usually drama-packed constests. He also believed that the paying customers preferred to see their favourites jousting for league and cup honours rather than watch some fanciful fare all dressed up and called Test Matches.

What came across was an apparent passionate desire to uphold the dignity of the competitors and, above all, the sport as a whole.

It did not find much favour among the gentlemen of the speedway Establishment who, in those days, were to be found at posh central London addresses such as the RAC Club in Pall Mall and the Speedway Control Board offices in Belgrave Square.

Basil's widow said: 'Speedway was just work as far as Basil was concerned. It was just a living – and a good living. But when a meeting was over he wanted to get away. There was no social life. Basil was what I call a man's man. He did not mix easily. He was an only child and quite used to being alone. He was never without a cigarette and he would never learn to drive a car.'

What Basil was really in love with, according to Rene, was journalism. He wrote, designed, laid out, edited and was there when they laid down the hot metal of the *Gazette* as it went to press. He was never nervous when he went to report a major meeting such as a World Final because he loved his job.

But just as the *Gazette* reached a peak of success in the mid-Fifties, the speedway boom which had taken place immediately after the war had begun to decline. Speedway started to fall out of favour with the public – and with it the *Gazette* as well.

In desperation they crammed in additional attractions. Film and showbiz news, saucy pin-ups, fiction. It just didn't work, and eventually Basil had no job. 'We just about survived,' said Rene.

I learned much later that Basil Storey 'wrote himself out of speedway.' It was a remark supposedly made by the then Control Board Manager, the sternly formidable ex-army Major W.W. 'Bill' Fearnley. The people who ran the sport did not like the frequent cutting public criticism of Basil's caustic comments which often held them up to ridicule and contempt.

As an example, this was typical of the invective he heaped upon the authorities in 1956 when, much as today, desperate attempts were being made to inject fresh appeal into a sport that was beginning to look as though it was on the road to ruin.

Under the headline 'This Scheme Won't Work', Storey wrote: *'In the name of sanity, what is this I hear about a Ronnie Greene scheme to revolutionise National League speedway racing?*

'Unless these old eyes and ears deceive me, the Wimbledon track chief wants four-team matches next season between four-men teams. A modified form of rider pooling is suggested to equalize the teams who will then operate in one league.

'In short, my esteemed friend Ronnie would seem to be proposing to go through the motions of picking up a tomato, wrapping it up and offering it for sale as a grapefruit. Well, this is me warning the undoubtedly well-meaning Ronnie, his fellow promoters and the Control Board in particular. The scheme won't work.'

Opposite: *Well, you have to start somewhere, and this was it (bottom of column two), my very first literary speedway effort and a mention in* Junior Speedway Gazette *from the man himself on 27 March 1948. It reads: 'I would particularly like to congratulate Master John Chaplin . . . on his effort entitled "The Eve Before The 1947 Riders Championship", which is a rather clever burlesque of Henry V's speech from Shakespeare's Before Agincourt.' It was signed Your Pal, Basil Storey. My Pal had an eye for talent . . .*

And this withering observation:

Pall Mall Pantomime Makes Me Weep . . . Control Board Study In Still Life!

'*Like the Gilbertian duke in* The Gondoliers *who led his regiment from behind because he found it less exciting, the Speedway Control Board continues to cry "Advance" and then immediately dive for safety into the dark cupboard under the stairs of its Pall Mall headquarters.*'

It was a report of a Control Board meeting to issue new track licences that Basil said had achieved absolutely nothing. He wrote: '*As usual, the Control Board . . . was surrounded by its bodyguard of promoters. It was the customary pantomime . . . unfortunately there was no cue in the script to prompt the pantomime fairy to dance through the door before the final curtain and announce* [a happy ending] *to the depressed Press boys waiting outside.*'

After more than half a century it all conjures up a strange feeling of *déjà vu*. The comments, you might consider, are a parallel of the situation in which speedway finds itself today.

For a while Two Gun Baz bummed around the other speedway magazines, the *News* and occasionally the merged *Speedway Star & News* – whoever would give him space. 'I have an outstanding weakness,' confessed Basil. 'I like to run things.'

Not many people know this, but Basil also played a mean piano – jazz and the classics. Between commissions he turned to trying to realize his real ambition. To see published a historical novel. Rene said: 'We had thousands of books. Basil was an intellectual, he liked the classics and the essayists: Defoe, Dickens, Macaulay, Shakespeare . . . '

So that's where the literary allusions came from.

But he failed. He never sold that historical novel. The dream never came true for Basil.

Through an old friend he eventually landed a job with the Press Association, finally becoming the racing editor. 'He hated every minute of it,' said Rene.

There have been occasions down the decades when I have had trouble dealing with Basil's desire to run things. I have been seated at my typewriter (before computers, that is) and somehow have been diverted from the task I set out to do into something completely different. I have attributed this phenomenon to the mischievous guiding hand of Basil from 'somewhere beyond the far unknown'.

Wherever he is, he can frown for all he is worth for all I care, but in spite of Rene's view that he cared not a jot for speedway racing, I am by no means certain she is correct. And this passage from Basil's writings may prove my theory. It is taken from his reaction to the Speedway Riders Championship Final at Wembley in 1947, won that year by Basil's washbuckling favourite, England's perennial crown prince, Jack Parker.

He reported: '*I thought I had seen everything and experienced all the emotions, until that vital Heat 8 when Pressmen rose screaming to their feet as Jack Parker beat Vic Duggan. The Australian was outwitted by England's famous Parker brotherhood.*

'*Vic led from the gate but for two laps had Norman Parker clinging to his tail. Jack was jogging long with tantalizing unconcern in third place, when suddenly, on the back straight of the third lap, with Vic concentrating on Norman, Jack came tearing through from the rear, flashing into the lead and, too late, Duggan realized he had been sold a dummy.*'

Basil referred to that most memorable of nights as 'the final rhapsody'. He said it was his greatest thrill.

So, where did I come into all this?

Well, it was on March 27th 1948. On Page 11 of *Junior Speedway Gazette* Basil published my first speedway literary effort. It was entitled: *The Eve Before The 1947 Riders Championship*, and it was based on the King's famous speech to his troops before the Battle of Agincourt from Shakespeare's *Henry V*.

I deliberately cribbed a bit of Shakespeare because I knew it would appeal to Basil.

It worked. And it set me on the road to here.

There is another tale that illustrates the whimsicality of the man. It seems that Mr Storey and Mr Morgan were in the habit of lunching once a week in the West End of London. Upon one of these occasions, in what at the time was described as 'a moment of unguarded fun', Mr Morgan ordered seven syrup puddings – a delicacy of which Mr Morgan and Mr Storey were particularly fond.

The waitress took Mr Morgan at his word and, having produced the seven syrup puddings, stood by while the shocked companions were compelled to clear all seven plates. Other diners thoroughly enjoyed the joke, and so too eventually did Mr Storey . . . it was Mr Morgan's turn to pay.

Basil Storey died on 5 July 1974 in a house in the village of Thropton, Northumberland. It is 37 miles due north from Brough Park where Newcastle Diamonds race – but it is a

SPEEDWAY GAZETTE, March 27, 1948—11

Junior Speedway Gazette

No. 35

DEAR JUNIORS.—In this issue of *JUNIOR SPEEDWAY GAZETTE* appear the final articles in our "1066 And All That" competition. Prize-winner this week is Master Donald Nudds, of 767, Cleckheaton Road, Oakenshaw, Bradford, Yorks.

The entries for this the final week of the competition were more numerous than ever and I had a difficult task selecting the winning article. I would particularly like to congratulate Master John Chaplin, of 173, Walstead Road, Walsall, Staffs, on his effort entitled "The Eve Before

Thanks for Writing

INTERESTING letters have been received from the following readers of JUNIOR SPEEDWAY GAZETTE :

Donald Freeman, 7, Hampden Road, Harrow Weald, Middlesex ; J. Budgen, 11, Downsway, Berwick Station, Nr. Eastbourne ; P. W. Tebbutt, 10, Fairway Avenue, Kingsbury, London, N.W.9 ; John G. Milburn, St. George's House, Otley Road, Harrogate, Yorks ; Ronald J. Crank, 15, Rutland Street, Leigh, Lancs ; Dennis Grabban, 26, Lonsdale Road, Notting Hill, London, W.11 ; Jack Marshall, 2, Western Avenue, Seaton Delaval, Northumberland ; Peter Alexander, 50, Killearn Street, Possilpark, Glasgow, N. ; John D. Taylor, 56, Cornwall Avenue, Southall, Middlesex ; Arthur West, 30, Grayshott Road, Battersea, London, S.W.11 ; J. A. Irwin, " Rose Dene," Church Road, Horsforth, Nr. Leeds, Yorks ; Freddie Boyce, 15, Kelmscott Crescent, Watford, Herts ; Graham Payne, 15, Locket Road, Wealdstone, Harrow, Middlesex ; Elsie Wilson, 112, Meath Road, West Ham, London, E.15.

The 1947 *Riders' Championship* " which is a rather clever burlesque of Henry V's speech from Shakespeare's " Before Agincourt."

Sheer comedy earns publication of " Wally Raleigh's Knighthood" by

16-year-old B. F. Scott, of 110, Hartley Road, Kingstanding, Birmingham, 22c.

And now, Juniors, let me be hearing from you in connection with Speedway Sam's new competition of which I published details last week. It is quite simple and really intriguing—a very short paragraph in which you are asked to incorporate the names of as many speedway riders as possible, such as : " Kitchen went into Lloyds Bank and asked the Clarke ' Howes the Price of Cole ? ', etc."

Please remember, boys and girls, to keep your paragraphs under 100 words in length. It won't be the length of your entry that will win you the cash prize but the number of riders' names you can work into the shortest paragraph.

By the time you read this we will have embarked on the 1948 speedway racing season and in closing my letter for this week I can once again return to my old formula by wishing you all cheerio for now—and good racing.

Your Pal,
BASIL STOREY.

An Oily Mess

By Donald Nudds

LET me tell you how Frank Drake and his Plymouth Angels came to invent the cinder track.

In the days of Queen Bess the Spanish Armada sailed to England. The Spaniards were upset at having lost the Test series to England by 5–0. Frank sighted the Armada off Plymouth Hoe but calmly continued practising on his new machine.

When he considered the Spaniards had drawn sufficiently close to England, Frank gave instructions to his Plymouth boys to clean all the oil from off their machines and pour it on the sea. The wily Drake then threw his cigarette-end into the sea and the oil blazed into a terrific inferno which reduced the Spanish fleet to a trail of cinders.

" Gadzooks ! " exclaimed Frank. " These cinders provideth me with a plan. From henceforth we will ride on cinders instead of Plymouth rocks."

Thus Drake invented the cinder track and was duly knighted at Pall Mall headquarters for his great service to speedway racing.

The Eve Before the 1947 Riders' Championship

By John Chaplin

THIS day is called September Eleventh ;
He that wins this day and gets the Cup,
Will stand a-tiptoe when the Eleventh is named,
And rouse him at the roar of a J.A.P.
He'll remember with advantages what 'eats he did to-day.

Then shall our names, familiar in their mouths as household words—
Parker (the Champ), Duggan and Longley, Kitchen and Wilks, Johnson and Wotton, be in their flowing cups freshly remembered ;
We sixteen, we happy sixteen, we band of rivals ;
For he to-day who shifts these cinders with me shall be my rival,
And this day shall gentle his condition and he shall be my brother.

Wally Raleigh's Knighthood

By B. F. Scott

IT was a dirty night in London on the occasion of the Old World Championship Final. Queen Bess toddled off to the Tower Stadium and, being rather short of cash, had to take her chance on the popular side.

Bess was delighted when her favourite rider Wally Raleigh won the Championship. As he flashed over the finishing line Bess hopped over the fence to congratulate him. She was about to step into a puddle in the centre of the track when Wally threw down his leathers to keep her feet dry.

" Coo . . . ta, awfully," gurgled Bess coyly, thrilled by her favourite's gallantry.

Wally bent his knee before the gracious Bess, who tapped him lightly on the shoulder with her rattle and cried for all to hear—" Arise, Sir Walter Raleigh ! "

million miles away from speedway. It is along a very beautiful valley, far from the cheering crowds and the world of men and motors.

Basil was terminally ill, and Rene recalls vividly his final words. She said: 'Any journalist will appreciate what they were. I remember I asked him how he felt, and he looked up and said: "Bloody awful."

'He would have loved that. He would have laughed like anything.'

Chapter 17

TOP GUNS

Back in the days when the big international high spots of the speedway season were the keenly fought Test matches between England and Australia, they knew how to tickle the sporting public's fancy with spicy pre-match publicity gimmicks . . . or at least Wembley did.

What you see here is the prelude to the 1933 series organised for the benefit of the press by Arthur Elvin and his cohorts at the Empire Stadium. Pictured are the two rival captains: on your left Victor Nelson Huxley of Australia, with his arm around that larger than life-sized cardboard kangaroo, and on your right Harold 'Tiger' Stevenson of England cuddling up to an equally unbelievably large lion.

Magazines and newspapers of the day showed Vic and the Tiger giving their national symbols a quick lick of paint in the middle of Wembley's sacred turf, before they went out to knock seven bells out of each other on the track.

It was the beginning of a tradition that saw Wembley stage the first of the annual five-

match series which was to last until 1938. This was an 18-heat match and scoring in the heats was 4 – 2 – 1.

The Australians were considered favourites to win because, though they had fewer big names to choose from, they were thought to be more determined than England. But amazingly they lost 47 - 76, as the big Wembley crowd was treated to lots of incident and controversy.

England's Ginger Lees set a new record by becoming the highest scorer in a Test with 21 points out of 24. In Heat 2 England's Claude Rye and Australia's Max Grosskreutz both crashed out of the match and were followed by England's Tom Farndon in Heat 8 and his team mate Wal Phillips in Heat 12. But home reserve Syd Jackson came to England's rescue with a fighting 15 points.

Eric Langton won four races for England. Then in his fifth he was disqualified for riding over the grass, and was so incensed that he threw a wobbly and refused to come out for his last ride. Tiger scored 13, Vic scored 12.

The series was eventually won by England by three matches to two. And when all the dust had settled the rival captains went off for a shooting holiday together. Though it does not seem to have been recorded who bagged the most.

Chapter 18

CAPTAIN AMERICA

Dateline: LOS ANGELES

THE man sitting beside me in the main stand at Costa Mesa suddenly got up, and I watched in amazement as he went down to the side of the track . . . and paid $500 for a quilt made up of speedway logos.

Just like that. Cool.

I wasn't even aware he had been bidding in what was an interval charity auction at the tiny, but legendary, West Coast speedway circuit just an hour's drive south of Los Angeles.

He returned to join me, at the 2001 US Final with a big grin on his face looking well satisfied. His company, an engineering firm, had, he explained, been planning to put in a similar amount in sponsorship money. So he was pleased that the cash was going to a good cause.

The man was Captain America 1952. Nick Nicolaides.

He had led the second great American invasion of British speedway just as the early post-war boom was beginning to fizzle out. The first American invasion of British speedway – leaving aside the great pioneers Lloyd 'Sprouts' Elder and Ray Tauser in the 1920s – had been in 1936 with the sensational arrival of Jack and Cordy Milne *(see page 80)*, and then Wilbur Lamoreaux a year later when they swept the World Championship board. Their contemporaries, Benny Kaufman and Miny Waln, had more muted success.

By the early Fifties, times – and attitudes – had changed. Whereas the Milnes, Lammy and the others had been warmly welcomed, the post-war scene was controlled largely by a closed shop riders' union, the Speedway Riders Association, which insisted on severely restricting the number of overseas riders appearing in British teams. Only Ernie Roccio at Wimbledon and Charles 'Pee Wee' Cullum at Belle Vue were allowed in.

And so it was that Wimbledon boss Ronnie Greene, who had been running a sort of 'Dons in exile' at Shelbourne Park, Dublin on Sundays, arranged for a full team from the United States to be resident at his Irish outpost in the 1951 season.

In the News From Abroad section in *Speedway World Monthly*, under the improbable byline of Fionnbar F. Callanan, there appeared this quote: 'A statement issued by the management of Shelbourne Park last week has been coolly received by many of the supporters of the Shelbourne Tigers.

'The statement was to the effect that next season the home team would be composed of the Americans whom Ronnie Greene is bringing over to Europe.

'This will mean that Ronnie Moore, Cyril Brine, Dennis Gray and the other Dons who became so popular last year will not appear this season except when the "New Tigers" oppose a Wimbledon team.

'Ernie Roccio, one of last year's Tigers, will be the only link with the past, and whether Messrs Nicolaides, (Chuck) Basney, (Royal) Carroll and Co can win the allegiance of the fans remains to be seen.

'I notice that one of the American riders bills himself as 'the best rider in the world'. I would advise this rider to leave it to the public to decide this question, at least while riding in Ireland, where self-praise is no praise!'

It was a reception that can only be described as . . . well . . . cool.

The experiment, by Greene, whose proud boast was that he could 'out-Hoskins Hoskins any time', was bold and revolutionary.

The influential *Stenner's Speedway Annual* reported in its 1951 edition that the Americans 'would probably be strengthened by the addition of old-timers Jack and Cordy Milne and Wilbur Lamoreaux during August and September'. It was a fanciful prophesy that was not to be fulfilled.

But the following season's annual recorded: 'The club tried the daring experiment of bringing to Dublin a team of riders from California to form the Shelbourne Tigers, and the gamble came off. At Dublin, those Tigers, assisted by Wimbledon American Ernie Roccio and sidekick Jimmy Gibb *(who was a Canadian)* built up an impressive record, beating Wimbledon twice, Belle Vue, Bristol, West Ham and Harringay. The only loss was to Coventry who were beaten on a subsequent return.

'England's C team, a Scottish Select and Norway also went down to the Americans who, however, could not hold Bruce Abernethy's fiery New Zealanders.

'Away the Tigers failed, sometimes miserably, but even so attracted some of the biggest gates of the British Division II season.

'Besides Ernie Roccio, the Americans had a stand-out in Nick Nicolaides. Johnny Roccio and Royal Carroll improved so much that a further season here could put them in the top class.'

Nicolaides topped the Americans' scoring in the series against England, his 64 points from the five matches was better than Ernie Roccio who scored 54 from four matches after missing one through injury. Nicolaides so impressed First Division New Cross boss Fred Mockford, who had the initiative and foresight to introduce the Milnes before the war, that he sought permission to borrow him for the Rangers' National Trophy engagements. But permission was refused.

The Americans were, however, allowed to compete in the World Championship qualifying rounds in England, Nicolaides failing by a mere two points to progress from the first round, with Don Hawley and Royal Carroll only just behind him.

Nick graduated to speedway from flat track racing in 1949, rising rapidly to challenge the accepted big stars, the Milnes, Lamoreaux and Gibb, in the West Coast stadiums around Los Angeles.

'I liked it, but I didn't know whether I could make a living at it,' said Nick.

In 1950 Ronnie Greene appeared and started to talk about taking a team back to Britain.

Doing the deal: Wimbledon chief Ronnie Greene in America meets some of the riders he arranged to base in Dublin in 1951. In the leather jacket, Ernie Roccio who was to become a star with Wimbledon, Chuck Basney shaking hands with Ronnie, and on the right Captain America Nick Nicolaides.

The perfect pair: Ernie Roccio (left) and Nick in the colours of the Dublin Tigers.

A young Nick: tickled to death to be invited.

The team, lined up at Liverpool: On the tour it included Royal Carroll, Lloyd Campbell, Johnny Gibson, Don Hawley, Jimmy Gibb, Ernie Roccio and Manuel Trujillo. Nick is holding the flag in the centre. Next to him is Johnny Roccio, Ernie's brother, and team manager Charles Arthur.

'I was invited to go and I was tickled to death,' said Nick. 'We raced in Dublin every Sunday and at least once a week in England. I used to get second half bookings at the English tracks, mostly Second Division. There was no deal as far as I was concerned. All I ever got out of it was my prize money – nothing extra.

'In 1952 Trevor Redmond invited me to go to South Africa in the British off-season, but I was on the verge of getting married and I didn't go. That was one of the reasons why I didn't progress any further in British speedway – because I was getting married. It seemed to me that if I was going to get married I shouldn't be racing speedway.

'When we rode in England as a team we were the American team in the American colours – Stars And Stripes race jackets. When we rode in Dublin we were the Dublin Tigers. Our colours were a green race jacket with a white star.

'We were each promised a new speedway bike when we got there – an Erskine Staride. We went to Wimbledon and checked in, and they had them all there. They kept their part of the deal.

'I remember one incident. I was at Fleetwood, and Wilf Jay was the captain. He was a tough guy. We were there, and as usual we didn't do too well the first time on the track. We were not allowed to practise. You ran up to the starting line, and that was it. We were losing and it was the last race of the night. Wilf Jay, myself, his partner Don Potter, and Royal Carroll were in it.

'The gate went up and we went into the first turn. Wilf and his partner had a half a wheel length on us. There was a tangle and I didn't have anywhere to go but off. So I was mad about it. I jumped up, grabbed my bike there in the middle of the track and just sat there. They had to stop the race, but of course they black flagged me and I didn't restart.

'So after several weeks we had the opportunity to go back to Fleetwood, and they had the exact same programme, rider for rider, heat for heat. I looked ahead to the last race, and there we were, all lined up again: Wilf Jay, Don Potter, me and Royal Carroll. But we were leading, and all we needed was one point to win the match. We could hardly lose.

'I was still carrying a grudge against Wilf Jay. So I said to Royal: "You just hang back. You are going to get at least one point out of this. Just hang back."

'Out of the start and into the first turn I was right behind Wilf. As we entered the back straightaway I just went up and took his leg and away he went. I got black flagged! But I got my own back. They carried him off but he wasn't hurt bad.'

'I got called before the racing board at the Auto-Cycle Union. It was very formal and they slapped my wrist. I got reprimanded. If I do that again . . . well look out.'

Nick recalled another time, at Coventry he said it was, when he remembers going into the first turn in one race and the next thing he was aware of was waking up in the shower. As he tells it, the handlebars on his bike had been fixed with the holding bolts being inserted bottom up with about three-quarters of an inch of bolt protruding. He crashed going into that first turn, lost consciousness and one of the bolts penetrated his helmet and split it.

Now, there is a picture of a helmet belonging to Nick that has been split. It appeared in the 1952 edition of *Stenner's Speedway Annual* and the caption read: 'When Nick Nicolaides, US star, crashed at Newcastle, a following rider ran over his head. Five minutes later Nicolaides got up, shook his head, and walked off unhurt. His crash helmet, top and side view, is shown above.'

Which could well have been another incident. In which case, Nick would appear to have led a charmed racing life in Britain.

But if most of his on-track activities were around the Second Division, Nick also mixed it with the big stars of the day on First Division circuits, taking on the likes of Aub Lawson, Bill Kitchen, Jack and Norman Parker, Ron Johnson, Wally Green, Split Waterman and Jack Young.

It was reported by a speedway journalist of the day that Nick's confessed burning ambition was to emulate Jack Young and win the world title. Was that an accurate quote. And, if so, why did he not go on to do it?

'Well,' said Nick. 'I guess I got sidetracked.'

The other thing I wanted to know was what had happened to Nick's American buddies after their two seasons in Britain.

'I guess that had we pursued it we could have come back. Because I felt that as a team we had been successful. In Dublin anyway. We had big crowds. The stands were packed. But also speedway wasn't really happening in the United States any more. I think that because so many of us came over to Britain the sport sort of died out at home.'

There was, of course, the tragic death in 1952 in a crash at West Ham of Ernie Roccio, the very popular next generation successful American after the Milnes and Lammy, who had emerged as world class the previous season by reaching the World Final. Did that have an effect on Nick's attitude to speedway?

'I was very saddened by it,' said Nick. 'Ernie and I were good friends. We were team riders together. He was very popular. We were talking about him only the other day –

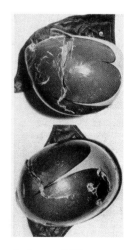

A charmed life: Nick's mangled helmet.

All set for action on their Staride bikes: From the left Johnny Roccio, Nick, Johnny Gibson (nicknamed Johnny Gumboil by Ronnie Greene because he had so many crashes) and Manuel Trujillo.

we've been talking about him for fifty years. His brother Johnny . . . he quit. It had a profound effect on Johnny and his family. He promised his mother he would never race again. And he never did. Johnny bench races now in the garage. And in bench racing you can go a lot faster than you do on the track!

'Ernie did well in the World Championship in 1951. That's a tough competition. I was at Wembley for that 1951 World Final. You know: Jack Biggs . . . ' It was of course the World Final Jack Biggs lost – sensationally. And – equally sensationally – the one Jack Young, of Second Division Edinburgh, won.

Jack needed one point from his final ride that night – to become World Champion. Before he left the pits for the fateful Heat 19, Jack did not seek any 'favours' from his three opponents, Split Waterman, Aub Lawson and Fred Williams. He was forced out on the first turn and trailed in last, then he came last in the three-man run-off for the title. A double whammy, you might say, for the little Australian.

Nick remembered: 'The story of the 1951 World Championship at Wembley Stadium was most memorable for me. I was there that night as a spectator. Of course I was cheering for my fellow countryman and good friend, Ernie Roccio. Ernie did not have a particularly good night but he was one of the 16 best speedway riders in the world that night and that is something to be proud of being.

'The race between Jack Young, Aub Lawson, Jack Biggs and Split Waterman was fantastic, I thought. Later at the banquet and dance upstairs at Wembley I had a quiet talk with Aub Lawson. That was a real eye-opener for me. I had met Aub early in the season at West Ham and we became friends. He told me about the deciding race, what really happened.

'Before that race Aub had approached Jack Biggs and asked him if he was "OK". According to Aub Jack just shrugged him off and turned away. Somehow that info got to the other two riders in that race and, well, we all know what took place on the track in that race.

'I knew that sort of thing went on. But mostly, in those days, it was straight-up racing. All season long. We enjoyed the physical thrill of racing – that's really what we were in it for. Four guys going into the first turn together and they're rubbing elbows and running over each other's feet . . .

    'It was a different time . . .

    'They were great days. I enjoyed them. The only regret I have is that I quit as soon as I did. I kind of wish now that I hadn't.

    'Yet, you know, if I'd continued I maybe wouldn't have the three children I have now, and my life wouldn't have turned out the way it has.

    'But it was probably the highlight of my life.'

Veterans' night out fifty years on at Costa Mesa: Manuel, Nick and Johnny Roccio remembering the great days.

WHAMO! THAT'S LIFE IN THE FAST LANE

EVEN at the age of seventy-five, Nick liked life in the fast lane. He and his partner Connie decided to take up Moto GP racing in California . . . until Nick missed a shift on his 750cc Suzuki taking a 100mph turn which resulted in him 'getting off pretty hard'.

    He was unconscious for twenty minutes and sustained a broken left clavicle, seven ribs and a punctured lung, which naturally put him in hospital.

    Meanwhile, Connie rode on.

    Nick decided he was too old for the discipline and they both switched to drag racing instead. He reckoned going in a straight line on a Hayabusa 180mph-190mph bike was safer.

    Not so.

    He hit the concrete wall and broke both wrists and his right ankle. Connie, in full flight, had to take swift avoiding action to miss the ambulance on its way to collect Nick.

    It was, he says, time to do something else – like land speed racing on a desert dry lake.

    'I managed 223.2mph.' says Nick. 'Connie did 217.0mph – she is a real competitor. When she has a good run she just lights up like a Christmas tree. At the Bonneville Speedway Week she would have hit over 240mph if she hadn't – whamo! – stripped the gear.'

    After Nick had a knee replacement, they were practising when Connie, seventy-one, had a 195mph crash, smashing her left clavicle, breaking both shoulder blades, nine ribs and two fingers on her left hand. *'Otherwise she was OK,'* says Nick.

    'During the off-season she healed OK, and in 2012, for my eighty-fifth birthday, she bought me a new Triumph Bonneville – a real nice bike.

    'We just recently bought a Honda Gold Wing 1830cc and sidecar. We got the sidecar because in 2011 Connie had to have a liver

Still loving living in the fast lane: Nick the twenty-first century hot shot.

transplant after a cancerous tumour was removed. She is recovering but it is taking time to regain her strength. We are going a little bit slower now and planning to ride to Florida for the Daytona 200.

'We then want to travel around our country and see some of the wonders of nature. I think it's about time.'

Right: *Two for the show – a bike show of course: Connie, the great competitor, and Nick*

Far right: *Laying it over, Nick No.532.*

Whamo! Connie chasing that elusive 240mph.

Chapter 19
THE SECOND NOEL

THERE is very little new under the speedway sun. True, old black/brown leather racing suits have evolved into today's grandiose multi-coloured kevlar creations (suits of lights?) you see plastered with sponsors' logos. Something 'modern' has also been done with the World Championship which means that today's fans will probably never know the magical atmosphere of a one-off World Final.

And should our friendly, dedicated devotees be under the impression that lay-down motors, as demonstrated in the action picture on the next page, are a twenty-first century phenomenon . . . they can think again.

For a start, the original speedway machine, the 1928 Dirt-Track Douglas, was horizontally mounted. And when pre-war England international and post-war mechanical guru Wal Phillips developed and refined the engine which dominated the sport for decades – the JAP – he came up with an inclined means of motive power as long ago as 1948.

That's him in the smart suit discussing technicalities with Jimmy Grant in the Harringay pits. And now, more than six and a half decades later, we can reveal how one of Britain's most accomplished restorers of speedway machinery, Noel Clark of Kidderminster in Worcestershire, has produced an exact replica of the Wal Phillips Special lay-down model.

That's it in the other picture over the page.

It is now part of his magnificent collection which includes Bradford and Bristol ace Fred Tuck's original OEC, Midland legend Dick Tolley's grasstrack machine and, once-upon-a-time, Belle Vue star and 1936 World No.2 Eric Langton's speedway bike.

Why did he do it?

Noel says: 'I wanted to wind up all these youngsters who think lay-downs have only just been invented. I know bikes don't get much attention from the fans, but I thought it would be interesting to show folks what Wal Phillips did all those years ago. I've no idea what happened to the original, but I built my replica in 1997. It took 12 weeks.

'I've built many speedway and grasstrack frames, so to make a good copy from photographs was not a big job. But there was a lot to do to the engine. The lubrication system had to be totally reworked, and the flywheel assembly balance altered to avoid vibration. It took quite some trouble to get that correct.'

Tell me if you can spot any differences between the Phillips and Clark masterpieces. Other than a slight difference in the rear engine plate, I can't.

Chapter 20
MIRACLE AT THE ZOO

By the late IVAN CROZIER

Dateline: Melbourne, Australia

NOW here's a thing. It's 1960-something-or-other, and the place is the Belle Vue track at Hyde Road, Manchester.

They called it The Zoo.

Peter Craven was top dog and could beat anybody he wanted to. We all were awed by this little bloke's skill on The Zoo's track. That's why they called him The Wizard of Balance

Now there was also Ronnie Moore, ready to retire but still blindingly fast and capable of great things. I was in the pit area, leaning on the fence like any other rider with a pass

Crossing the wetline 1: Peter Craven pays the penalty of missing the gate to a 'still blindingly fast' Ronnie Moore at The Zoo.

Crossing the wetline 2: it's total wipeout for The Wizard Of Balance, and Mirac, still capable of great things, never loses a yard.

to get in. On my right was Dick Fisher, on my left Cyril Maidment. And Craven missed the gate but was beside Moore into the first turn.

Maidment said: 'Oh, shit!' and moved away. Dick Fisher went with him.

What had happened?

Craven and Moore went down the back straight as one – as I knew they would. I'm not a fool. I had seen Craven bury champions before. Manchester was where I lived. Craven was the king of Manchester.

Then both crossed the wet line that always went from the pit area down onto the track, and Ronnie never lost a yard – but Peter Craven did.

That was the difference. That was why Fisher and Maidment walked away.

That was why they called Ronnie Moore Mirac!

I had never seen it before. It was only then that I understood.

Chapter 21
THE SENSATIONAL STENNERS . . .

SPEEDWAY is a few scandals short of a sensation. Once upon a time this great sport of ours used to be stuffed with sensations – thanks to the likes of Kenny Carter, Bruce Penhall, Michael Lee, Split Waterman, Graham Warren, Billy Lamont, Vic Duggan, Johnnie Hoskins, Vic Huxley, Phil Bishop, Dick Case, Putt Mossman, Harold 'Tiger' Stevenson, Jack Parker, Eric 'Rickey' Chitty, Frank Arthur, E.O. Spence and Tom Bradbury-Pratt.

Need I go on?

Well, yes, I need, actually.

Why?

Well, first, because I am well aware that some of those names just might be a trifle unfamiliar to some of you, especially if you are among – shall we say – the more recent generations of speedway fans.'

So I should explain that every one of them wrote a major chapter in speedway history – either as a rider or as a promoter. One of them, Roarin' John Hoskins, claims to have invented the whole thing – and never stopped roarin' about it until the day he died in his nineties.

Quite right, too.

Sensations and scandals were the staff of life to every one of them, especially Hoskins. If there were no sensations going, Johnnie manufactured a few.

My second reason for going on is because there is one very important name missing from that extremely distinguished and historic dirt-track line-up.

The name is Tom Stenner.

Now Tom Stenner was a speedway writer. And a doyen among them, to boot.

A doyen is defined as a senior member of a group or profession. And in the profession of speedway journalists – sometimes disparagingly referred to as 'The Mucky Mackintosh Brigade' – Tom Stenner was undoubtedly a doyen.

Mr Sensation Chicago style: Tom Stenner, purveyor of red hot news and amazing scoops.

I am bringing Mr Stenner to your notice because on this occasion I wish to direct the spotlight in the direction of the Gentlemen (and I use the term 'Gentlemen' very advisedly) who were once known as the Fourth Estate, who preferred to conduct their activities clad in green eyeshades and shirt-sleeve suspenders, were permanently attached to their local bar by one elbow, their typewriters by two fingers and spent much of their working lives going around shouting: 'Hold the front page!' (*See also The Secret Life Of Basil Storey, page 108).*

You've got it. The Press.

I left out the word 'gutter' because Mr Stenner was a few rungs higher than the gutter. He was the Speedway Correspondent of the upmarket *Daily Mail* and, by his own unabashed and less than modest admission, a bit of a Godsend to the sport. He had an office in the confines of the magnificent Harringay Stadium which, in his day, was a serious rival as a sporting and entertainment centre to the Wembley complex in neighbouring

VOL. I. No. I.   NOVEMBER, 1935.

TOM STENNER MAGAZINE

SPEEDWAY

Hold the front page. Smiling through Volume 1 Number 1, the unabashed and less than modest Editor.

North London. He was therefore in daily touch with the year-round happenings in speedway racing during the summer and ice hockey in the winter, together with such things as boxing matches and musical events.

The Stenners – Tom and Jim (I never knew whether Jim was Tom's son or brother) – are best remembered for the unique nine-volume series of *Stenner's Speedway Annuals* published between 1946 and 1954, which are rightfully now valuable collectors' items and head any serious speedway memorabilia student's must-have shopping list.

Tom also wrote the definitive speedway commentary, *Thrilling The Million: The Lure Of The Speedway,* in 1934, and vintage Pop fans will no doubt be amazed to learn that its publishers, John Miles Ltd, gave their address as Amen Corner, which was a location in London EC4, and nothing whatever to do with the Welsh rock group led by Andy Feairweather-Low.

I'm telling you all this because, comparatively recently, there came into my possession a slim volume of Mr Stenner's work about which, hitherto, I had known nothing. It was a very slim volume indeed – a bound collection of five monthly journals published over the winter of 1935-1936 entitled *the Tom Stenner Magazine* – or TSM as it seemed to prefer to be known. And, since you ask, no I had never heard of the TSM before launching the *Vintage Speedway Magazine* which became popularly known as VSM.

You'll pardon me for saying so, but *the Tom Stenner Magazine* wasn't a very imaginative title, and I had to do a fair amount of research to establish the exact publishing date because whoever had the series bound had thoughtfully removed the covers and there was, consequently, no indication of dates.

The giveaway came in the third issue. There was a black bordered panel at the bottom of page 3. There, Stenner had written: 'On behalf of 2,000,000 speedway followers we humbly tender our heartfelt sympathy to Her Majesty Queen Mary and the Members of the Royal Family on their irreparable loss. Their grief is our grief because King George was one of us . . .'

He was acknowledging the death of King George V who, at seventy, had died at Sandringham on 20 January.

But, in an editorial above, illustrated with a picture of a beaming Stenner in wide-brimmed fedora, Chicago-gangster style, he announced that the public reception of his new monthly had been so sensational it was to become a weekly from the first speedway meeting of the new season in April.

Note that, customers. In those days no tapes rose until at least April, so putting the boys in no danger of having to brush away snow from their goggles as has been known to happen in more recent times.

The phones, said Stenner, had been ringing off their hooks, the postman could hardly lift the sacks of appreciative letters. Never before, not even in his long experience of journalistic and literary production, had a magazine, whatever its nature, received such an amazing welcome.

It was, he implied, his bounden duty to 'gladly bow to public opinion (and) do our share to help this great family of followers of the greatest sport in the world to get away from the often drab and unromantic realities of life by (bringing them) vivid, colourful and intimate stories of the game of thrills by red hot news and amazing journalisitic scoops . . .'

It sounded like *Mission Impossible* to me, but he didn't let down that great speedway public.

In the short run of the magazine, contained within the green leather covers I counted no fewer than nine sensations, seven shocks, four scandals, one bombshell, one snub, a slight and one out-and-out tragedy.

Stenner kicked off with the great *Crash Hat Scandal*. And the journalistic style had a definite touch of the modern red-tops about it. In Volume 1 Number 1 the lead story went like this:

'DEATH stalks the flying wheels of the speedway rider. I do not refer to the risks inseparable from the sport, but to risks that need not and should not be taken and have left a wake of crippled lives.'

The substance of the story was that riders were tempting fate by wearing 'obsolete or useless helmets that are a menace and not a protection. Many a rider has retired from the track broken in mind and body after a heavy fall, yet would be riding today but for a useless helmet.'

Was this a sensation, or what?

He cited Wembley's George Greenwood who had scrapped a cork-lined helmet for a sorbo rubber-lined one after several alarming crashes, and Stenner went on to warn the Control Board and the speedway managements of the dire consequences to come unless something was not done to standardise helmets.

Next came a *U.S.A Bombshell*. Under a Los Angeles dateline. There followed a story that the American speedway authorities were anxious to send a national Test team to England. 'Suggestions that American riders are not good enough to compete with English stars has caused much resentment . . . and there is a widespread feeling of indignation at the slight,' went the report. 'It's about time John Bull gave us a break!'

Uncle Sam having a go at John Bull, indeed!

Likely starters included Jack and Cordy Milne, former Wimbledon favourite Ray Tauser, Byrd McKinney and Wilbur Lamoreaux, with former super pioneer speedway showman Lloyd 'Sprouts' Elder as team manager.

They were names that were shortly to blaze across the speedway firmament – but not in an American Test side.

Another 'Sensation'. This time at Sydney. 'Hansen Crashes – Women Faint' roared the headline. The story was that Dane Morian Hansen's eagerly anticipated appearance in Australia had been prefaced by fanfares of trumpets. But in a match race with England's Herbert 'Dusty' Haigh he had picked up drive, struck Dusty's rear wheel and turned 'several sorts of somersaults' before colliding with the safety fence head-on.

'So keyed up were the crowd with all the excitement, that scores of women screamed and fainted. Several did not recover until receiving hospital treatment,' reported a 'Special Correspondent'. Morian copped a 'beautiful black eye' and went to hospital but was not detained.

And then there was quite the most amazing speedway story I have ever read. The headline announced: *Pall Mall Copy Pisa*. This was an account of how the experimental department of the Speedway Control Board, then based in London's Pall Mall, were planning a weekend visit to view the famous Tower of Pisa in Italy 'to see how that tower was leaning.'

Because – and I kid you not, customers – the idea was to eliminate the danger of the starting tapes catching a rider and unseating him from his machine as they rose straight up. The SCB panjandrums thought that by inclining the starting gate posts backwards, a la Leaning Tower of Pisa, the tapes would go up – and back – and thereby not sweep a rider from his bike.

But, observed the TSM: 'It is a long way to the new season and maybe they will have thought of another bright idea by then.'

Quite.

In my opinion, Mr Stenner was being incredibly, indulgently gentle with a collection of Control Board loonies. Unless, of course, in true modern tabloid tradition, he had made the whole thing up.

What other delights had we in store?

Well, there was a suggestion for – have we been this way recently? – *A New Wembley*. The TSM had learned of plans to enlarge the speedway track at the Empire Stadium, at an expenditure of at least £5,000. By moving back the greyhound course, 'a not too difficult operation', there would be space for a complete quarter mile cinder track.

The idea, quoth TSM, would do away with the need to remove part of the soccer pitch at the start of each speedway season. Now, when you think about it my friends, wouldn't that have been the salvation of speedway at Wembley and wouldn't it have done away with all the subsequent ill-feeling and resentment the mechanical sport has had toward the Football Association for depriving it of its spiritual home? And wouldn't it have prevented all that antagonism the soccer supremos directed at speedway racing for allegedly

*Hats off to Mr
Stenner. Well, he
seems to have
forsaken his fedora to
be part of the VIP
line-up in the
reflected glory of
Charles Eade,
Editor of the old*
Sunday Dispatch,
*sponsor of the early
post-war World
Championships.*

knocking their sacred turf about?

It was quite the most sensible item the magazine had come up with thus far.

There was another feature that caught my eye. It was by legendary Belle Vue chief E.O. Spence and was headlined: *What I Have – I Hold!*

The opening paragraph revealed all: 'For the past three seasons my team, Belle Vue Manchester, have been top of the speedway world and have won every honour the sport has to give. This continued success has set London managements by the ears and for some time now it has been broadly hinted that Belle Vue are far too strong and that some of our riders should be released to strengthen other clubs. . .

'On a recent visit to London I was dragged into a managerial conference that lasted until the early hours and almost given the third degree in an effort to make me disgorge – as it was put – my overplus talent. It is for the good of the sport, I was told.'

Well, old E.O. was having none of it.

He had released a star the previous season, he said. The brilliant Frank Charles had been allowed to go to Wembley. In Manchester, he pointed out, they had found and trained their own riders, whereas other managements had the whole of London to choose from.

'No,' insisted E.O., 'what I have I hold. I will not release a single rider – not a cinder! That team of go-getters called Belle Vue I mean to keep. It is up to the other managements to find their own salvation.'

And he finished with a sucker punch.

'To be quite frank,' he said, 'the real reason for the non-success of London clubs when meeting Belle Vue is that they are obsessed with an inferiority complex!'

Ha, ha! So there!

What, I wonder, would happen today if some iron-willed speedway entrepreneur decided to waive such an uncompromising red rag in front of his bullish fellow promoters?

The TSM, though, was first to break the news of the introduction of an official World Championship due to be staged in 1936. Describing it as 'the greatest speedway competition ever devised', the news was that there would be a first prize of £500 and a total of more than £2,000 for the whole competition, which would include 'representatives of every country where the sport of thrills holds sway.'

The TSM *Exclusive* went on: 'This competition promises to be (wait for it) the *SENSATION* of the century'.

There it is again – yet another sensation!

Johnnie Hoskins (West Ham) was apparently the 'prime mover' of the project and, with a working committee made up of Alec Jackson (Wembley) and Cecil L. Smith (New Cross), he was to finalise the details. The World Championship was to replace the British Championship, suspended after the death of reigning title holder Tom Farndon *(see page 64)*, and the old Star Championship. It was, speculated TSM, 'the chance of a lifetime to put speedway on the map forever'.

A little further on, what do we find?

You guessed it. Yet another sensation.

They just kept coming, didn't they?

This one was a *Sensational Star Grabbing Plot*, and told the tale of a dastardly scheme 'to deprive England of her leading speedway riders and take them on a three year world tour.'

The idea was apparently 'backed by influential men from every walk of life – there is not a speedway official interested – (and) the scheme is being financed by a £250,000 syndicate.'

Plans were in hand, reported TSM, for this world tour to begin at the end of the present (1936) English season with 20 stars from British tracks. 'Such men as Eric Langton, Vic Huxley, Max Grosskreutz, Bluey Wilkinson, Jack Parker, Frank Charles, Dick Case, Ron Johnson, Tiger Stevenson, Bill Kitchen, Lionel Van Praag, Jack and Cordy Milne and Eric Chitty would be invited.'

The names were the cream of contemporary world speedway and represented just about anybody who was anybody in the sport. It appears to me to be suspiciously similar to a latter day formula for a Grand Prix series.

Doesn't bear thinking about, does it?

That sensation – such as it was – appeared on page 26 of the 30-page final edition in my bound volume, and seems to have been the swansong of TSM. For, try as I might, I have found no further issues.

Those sensation soaked pages had also announced that Hollywood had gone Cinder Crazy with famous film stars, including Clarke Gable, Joe E. Brown, Robert Montgomery and Jean Harlow going mad for speedway.

THAT Harringay had offered a 'stupendous' £7,000 for the Belle Vue Ace Max Grosskreutz, which would 'put speedway transfer fees on a par with football'; that 'Death Stalks New West Ham Star' on a story that Canadian Eric Chitty had been given up for dead twice after 'terrible crashes'.

THAT England's Wally Lloyd and Phil Bishop had joined the board of a big syndicate to establish speedway in Johannesburg in a 'South African Sensation' (what else?).

THAT Wembley's 'Whirlwind Van Praag' had taken New Zealand speedway by storm in an All Nations International at Wellington.

THAT at the same location, 18,000 spectators had looked on in horror when they saw 'one of the most terrible accidents the sport has ever known. The victim was a charming and beautiful girl, a well-known Hollywood beauty who has appeared in many films.' Daredevil American Putt Mossman had misjudged a motorcycle stunt when roaring blindfold up a ramp 'no more than a foot wide' and landed on his unfortunate prone wife Helen who he had been supposed to hurdle at speed. Mrs Mossman was removed unconscious to hospital suffering from severe internal injuries and a broken arm.

Every story a little gem, and all – of course – sensational stuff.

In one editorial 'The Editor' (that is, Tom Stenner), was at pains to point out: 'Modesty is a becoming garment . . . but just to put you all in personal touch . . . let's drop the editorial "we" for the more intimate "I".'

Back in the early days, he went on, speedway was practically ignored by Fleet Street. 'Well,' he confessed, 'I gave a hand to put that right. In those early days, too, promoters were on the point of throwing league racing overboard . . . I'm glad I helped to persuade them to stand by the league, which has proved the backbone of the sport.

'It also fell to my lot to introduce some of the big Cup and Trophy competitions, and to play a big part in the institution of Test matches between England and Australia. Every rider is a personal friend; I have been godfather to the children of married ones and the confidant of the unmarried.

'But,' insisted the incredible Mr Stenner, 'it's the game that counts and not the individual.'

Oh, really? Four cheers for Mr Stenner!

Yet in spite of all the 'red-hot news and vivid stories' that his magazine carried – not to mention the ten-a-penny SENSATIONS – what happened to the weekly edition, and its promise to 'put a new urge into our national life'?

It does not appear to have seen the light of day.

A sensation in itself?

Chapter 22

BY GEORGE . . . IT'S THE HOUNDS

FROM out of the past, this band of happy warriors blazed a trail briefly, but brightly, across the speedway firmament.

They are the Tamworth Hounds who for a mere four years raced at their picturesque track at nearby Fazeley, deep in the heart of Staffordshire hunting country – hence their nickname, the Hounds.

The man in the funny hat pushed them off on April 30 1947. You probably won't recognize him without his little ukelele in his hand – it's the popular entertainer George Formby and his wife Beryl getting captain Steve Langton going at the opening meeting. With a little help from colourful promoter Arthur 'Westy' Westwood.

And just check out the smart get-up worn by the pusher-off on the left with his neat beret, sparkling white pants and sweater emblazoned with the Tamworth Hound. You don't see pushers-off attired like that these days. What's the betting he could march in step, too?

Westy was one of the legendary – and rascally – pioneer swashbucklers of the sport, (that's him again in the smart suit in the centre of the team picture). His Hounds were only a Third Division outfit, beginning their short career in the newly-formed league in 1947,

but Westy had gathered, within their ranks, a wealth of speedway history and folk lore and talent.

For instance, on the left is Charlie Oates, the idol of – and who later nurtured – the late, great Peter Craven. Next to him, Ted Gibson who helped carry the speedway gospel to South Africa, and Cyril Page, who skippered Stoke and later Leicester, serving Birmingham with distinction too.

Next to Westy is the Australian veteran Steve Langton, one of the pioneers of the sport from way back in the early 1930s, then comes Bill Harris, one of two racing brothers, and Fred Yates, probably the only schoolteacher-speedway rider who raced for England.

On the left at the front, Jack Baxter, who later became the second husband of Muriel Wilkinson, the widow of 1938 World Champion Bluey Wilkinson. And finally Arthur Payne, then a young Australian who went on to be a World Finalist and have a star-spangled international career with Birmingham.

Those original race jackets of blue and white halves with a red hound were eventually replaced by a red 'T' on a yellow background when the club became part of Birmingham boss Les Marshall's Midlands speedway empire. They raced their last in 1950.

And after more than sixty years there is no sign a track ever existed there. It has been replaced by houses on what is now known as Deer Park Road.

Blazing the trail: Arthur Payne (left) and Charlie Oates setting the pace for the Hounds .

Chapter 23
CACKLE

THIS dashing young man never set out to be a speedway rider at all. His early ambition was to be a trumpet player, but a road accident which injured his lips wrecked that career. So he took to the track, inspired by being allowed to carry the leathers of his hero, pre-war West Ham and England star Colin Watson.

He is Ilford born Malcolm Craven, known to the entire speedway world as Cackle, because of his raucous laughter. Watson taught him the basics of the cinders game at the old Dagenham track. Eventually Alec Jackson signed the young Craven for Wembley, loaning him out to first Norwich and then Birmingham in the old Second Division.

But Craven was destined for the top. Recalled by Wembley in 1939, he made such rapid progress that he qualified as reserve for that year's World Final which was never held because of the war.

Destined for the top. The dashing young Malcolm proudly displaying that distinctive, sought after Wembley sweater.

After service in the Merchant Navy, he joined his old idol Watson at West Ham in 1946, finishing fifth in the British Final at Wembley. He had a distinctive action style and, when all about him were switching to high, wide and handsome cowhorn handlbars, Cackle always stayed faithful to his narrow downturned ones.

At one time he had a jeweller's shop in London, he was a qualified pilot – that's also him in his flying suit – and he often flew himself to meetings. He stayed with West Ham until the end of his career in the mid-Fifties, latterly riding in flamboyant gold coloured leathers, before retiring to Canada.

Notes: Belle Vue rider Stan Hart was killed on 25 August 1937 in the Hall Green Speedway in Birmingham. Hart fell and was hit by the machine of Birmingham competitor Malcolm Craven. The meeting was immediately abandoned.

Flying low. The unmistakably cool and sophisticated Craven style. Malcolm at speed passing the West Ham pits.

Far left: *On his way . . . young Craven has already landed a brace of trophies, so maybe he can be forgiven for wanting to blow his own trumpet . . . even if a road accident prevented him making a career of it.*

Left: *Flying high: Malcolm the aviator in his pilot's kit.*

Chapter 24
THE BOMBSHELL

Genius on a Speedway Bike

SPEEDWAY'S Old Guard was beginning to fade away. The great and glorious pre-war names – Jack and Norman Parker, Ron Johnson, Vic Duggan, Bill Kitchen, Tommy Price, Eric Langton and the rest of the pioneer veterans – were still good, still drawing the crowds. But a bright new post-war generation of young pretenders was on the rise.

Leading the way were Fred Williams, Dent Oliver, Split Waterman, Louis Lawson and Cyril Roger. They were to be followed by Ken LeBreton, Ronnie Moore, Jack Young, Alan Hunt and Barry Briggs.

But before them a bombshell was to shake the speedway world to its very foundations in the shape of a golden-haired, self-possessed, handsome young man of twenty-two who soared like a comet to superstardom virtually overnight.

He was the Blond Bombshell. Otherwise Mr Dynamite. Graham Warren.

Born in Fiji, he was possessed of so much remarkable talent that there are not enough superlatives to put before the name Graham Warren. Yet, as one of many young hopefuls fresh in from the other side of the world in 1948, no one in Britain wanted to know him.

But within weeks, it seemed the entire speedway world was at his feet. His aggressive, exciting, explosive style – the length of the straight on his back wheel, no problem, and he wasn't showboating – mesmerised and thrilled the terrace fans wherever he went.

Though born in Fiji he was raised in Sydney. His heroes were the great pre-war Australian stars, Max Grosskreutz, Lionel Van Praag and Bluey Wilkinson, and he learned to ride motorcycles as a despatch rider in the RAAF during the war.

His early speedway record in Australia amounted only to winning the Bluey Wilkinson Memorial Shield at Bathurst on a machine that once belonged to Ray Duggan. A chance meeting with former Harringay team manager John Deeley resulted in a scribbled note of introduction and he set off to find fame and fortune in England along with another Australian hopeful, Ern Brecknell, who had a contract from West Ham.

At Custom House they wouldn't even give Graham a trial ride. But from Norman Parker, one of the fading stars he was soon to challenge and who later became the best man at Graham's fabulous, traffic-stopping wedding, he heard that Birmingham promoter Les Marshall was looking for talent for his Third Division Cradley Heath side.

I was one of a bunch of ragged-trousered, utterly awestruck schoolboys, who had somehow managed to sneak into the 'posh' car park on the expensive (2s 6d adult, 1s 3d child) side of the terracing at the Alexander Sports Stadium, Perry Barr, Birmingham.

What we were after was the autographs of our heroes: Stan Dell, our captain, Doug McLachlan, our recent signing from Newcastle, Dick Tolley, the famous Midlands grass track ace, Roy Dook, one of the early pioneers from way back and a skilful leg-trailer of the old school, and Charlie May, who had actually ridden for the famous Wembley Lions.

I distinctly remember a slim young man, with a head of glamorous-looking golden hair, coming to the railings where we were, taking my autograph book and without even looking at me, signing his name in it. When he handed it back to me the name that he had written was 'Graham Warren'.

I showed it to my friends: 'Graham Warren?' we said. 'Who is Graham Warren?'

We soon found out.

We had just met the Blond Bombshell who, in his first meeting for Cradley, a challenge match at Tamworth, had shown his extraordinary ability from the start, scoring 11 points

Above left: *The young pretender has arrived . . . Graham, in his Australian sweater (he was intensely patriotic) made such progress in his first season, 1948, that he was selected to challenge his Birmingham captain, Stan Dell, for the Second Division Silver Helmet Match Race Championship. Graham took the title.*

Above centre: *The Bombshell is besieged. What the speedway star of the late forties wore to meet his fans, Graham in immaculate suit and tie.*

Above right: *Mr Box Office. It was because of Graham that Birmingham got the call to join the First Division in 1949. The team at Wimbledon is, from the left, Arthur Payne, Brian Wilson, Buck Whitby, Geoff Bennett, Dick Tolley, Graham, Wilbur Lamoreaux and Doug McLachlan.*

Left: *World class: Graham before the first Test of 1949 at Wembley. He helped Australia to a very convincing 57 – 41 win with an unbeaten 18-point maximum.*

The 1948 Second Division Birmingham superteam that Graham helped project into the big time. Standing from left, George Buck (manager), Doug McLachlan, Geoff Bennett, Stan Dell, Dick Tolley, Roy Dook and promoter Les Marshall. Kneeling: Buck Whitby, Charlie May and Graham.

out of a maximum of 12 and breaking the track record by almost two seconds.

I watched him win three second half races at Birmingham, including a victory over home skipper Stan Dell, which convinced Les Marshall that Graham was too good for Division Three so he put him in his Division Two team at Perry Barr – and the Cradley fans never forgave him.

Progress was then so meteoric that soon West Ham were offering £4,000 for the young upstart they rejected – more than the record transfer fee they eventually paid Edinburgh for World Champion Jack Young.

By then Graham was the sensation of the Second Division, an Australian Test star, Division Two Match Race Champion, and the inspiration that lifted a lack-lustre Birmingham side into National Trophy giant killers, ironically scalping Division One leaders West Ham by a virtual cricket score: 85 – 23 at Perry Barr.

It was the Warren machismo that earned the Brummies promotion to the First Division the following season. That and the fact that they had a super central stadium with a 40,000-plus capacity.

So outstanding was Graham, scoring 25 maximums in that first year, that all nine journalists invited to rank the division's top rider put him at number one.

The powerful critic Basil Storey *(see page 108),* Editor of *Speedway Gazette,* the first to call Graham the Blond Bombshell because of his golden locks and Mr Dynamite because of his impact on the sport, wrote: 'Warren's brilliance put him in a class of his own.'

Suddenly, everybody wanted Graham. Every week, tempting offers came his way. From Wembley, Wimbledon, Belle Vue and Harringay. 'Especially Harringay,' Graham once told me. Harringay was where he made his international Test debut for Australia in August, winning his first ride from partner Bill Longley and England's Split Waterman and Alec Statham.

He recalled: 'I think the biggest in-my-pocket inducement I was offered was £1,000.' It was fabulous money in those days – £22,500 in today's values. But Graham turned it down to stay loyal to Birmingham. After all, he had made Birmingham. . . and Birmingham had

The Warren first World Final at Wembley in 1949. From the left the line-up is: Bill Gilbert, Dent Oliver, Aub Lawson, Graham and eventual winner Tommy Price. It wasn't a happy debut for Graham: he finished 12th on five points – but it was to be very different the following year.

made him.

Storey wrote: 'Realising that he meant Box Office, London promoters began falling over themselves to book Graham for their star-studded second half events. Warren showed his appreciation by setting up an all-time record by winning his first race on each London track he visited. In an era of one-track riders, Warren proved himself little short of a Miracle Man.'

Within the year, Graham had proved himself world class. Not only had his brilliance elevated Birmingham to the premier division but he was nominated to challenge the match race master, Jack Parker, for the legendary Golden Helmet. Parker, at the time, was ranked third in the world behind Graham's fellow Australians Vic Duggan of Harringay and Ron Johnson of New Cross. And 43,000 people paid to see their clash at Perry Barr.

The established international: Graham with veteran Tommy Price.

Such was Graham's popularity that his wedding brought the entire centre of Birmingham to a standstill. The occasion attracted as big a crowd as the nuptuals of a television soap star would today.

The very finest Warren hour came at the 1950 Wembley World Final when he came within touching distance of speedway's ultimate prize, the World Championship. He was unbeaten in four rides, but in Heat 10, his third ride, he fell challenging eventual winner, home hero and Wembley expert Fred Williams. That one single, fateful slip snatched the title from him.

Graham once described the incident to his son Mark, who said: 'Graham was going to drive under Freddie Williams not round him, he didn't want to run into him (he didn't like running into anyone), so he eased off a little, the bike straightened up and down he went. When you're really moving that sort thing can happen! In a split second you're on your arse. Graham was no strategist, it wasn't in his racing nature to just sit there.'

At the time he was without peer, the best speedway rider in the world. Even after the Wembley disaster he topped the world rankings above Parker and Aub Lawson. New champion Williams was placed sixth.

Graham was never to be so close to the world title again. That winter, a near fatal accident during a handicap race at Palmerston North in New Zealand robbed him of much of his dash and fire. And though he made a comeback, the outstanding brilliance was gone.

There were more crashes, and his beloved Birmingham closed following the death in South Africa in 1957 of the man who had taken over his mantle as Mr Birmingham, Alan Hunt, with whom he had a less than amicable relationship.

Sensation at West Ham: Graham challenging Aub Lawson in the first leg of the 1948 National Trophy clash which saw Second Division giant killers Birmingham scalp the First Division league leaders.

But still Graham came back, and appeared in Coventry's colours, eventually ending his racing career with Provincial League Wolverhampton – a long, long way down from the pinnacle he had reached, it seemed, without much effort because he had such a monumental gift for racing a speedway machine.

Off the track, Graham could be on occasions difficult and acerbic, but in his own way he dedicated his life to the sport that very nearly took it from him that night in New Zealand. I once asked him why he did it, and he said: 'I came back because I was dyed-in-the-wool speedway. Maybe it was a mistake on my part and I should have kept right out of it, but I had to ride . . .

'The thing I'll never forget about my career is chasing Freddie Williams and falling on my ear. And one of the nicest things was being chosen as captain of my country in a Test match in Australia. I felt very proud. It was a patriotic thing.'

Mark Warren says: 'Graham had loved cycle racing his entire life from the age of eight. He returned to pushing pedals at amateur level in his late forties and won many major track events, competing regularly in road races. He was a great hill climber and was in fact a natural athlete and born racer. At the age of fifty-four he rode in the Goulburn to Sydney race – 120 miles, 120 starters – finishing 58th. Not bad when you consider that most of the competitors were half his age.'

My last meeting with Graham was arranged by his old Birmingham team mate and friend Arthur Payne. He was living in a war veterans' home on Queensland's Gold Coast. His home bore little evidence of the glory days. There was only the giant silver bowl he won by beating the great Jack Parker at Walthamstow in 1950 – he won nearly everything in 1950, apart from the title that mattered – and a World Final race jacket, cracked with age draped over the back of a chair. I was gratified to notice, that a tribute to him I had written some time before, had been framed and presented to him by Ivan Mauger, who regarded him with some reverence.

The super stylist at home: Graham leads Oliver Hart, Ken LeBreton and Jack Parker at Sydney in the second Test of the 1949-50 series.

Graham had become a pale shadow of the vibrant glamour boy I had first encountered, the thunderbolt who rattled the cages of speedway's top names. Over tea and biscuits I asked him what he thought of speedway now. 'I'm biased,' he said. 'It's nothing like it used to be. Nowadays they are nowhere near as good as we were.'

The Blond Bombshell passed the final chequered flag in 2004 at the age of seventy-eight. Mark described Graham's final days: 'I cared for Dad in the last month of his life, so he died at my home in Possum Creek at Bangalow on the far north coast of New South Wales. My brothers Leigh and Kym were present.

'My father meant a great deal to me, I didn't want him to die amongst strangers in some nursing home. I loved him dearly from my earliest memories to this day, even with his shortcomings! But there was plenty more to him than those.'

'Shortcomings'?

Graham at times could be irascible, impatient and hot-tempered, a trait often considered the attribute of genius – and it would not be too fanciful to describe Graham Warren as a genius on a speedway machine.

There has been only one Blond Bombshell, and as long as there is speedway the name can only ever mean one man. The original. Graham Warren.

A winning night at Walthamstow. Actress Rosalind Boulter presents Graham with a handsome trophy in 1950 – the year Graham was ranked number one in the world.

EVENT 15, PALMERSTON NORTH

FEW details of Graham's accident, ironically on 13 January 1951, at Palmerston North have ever been published, apart from the fact that it resulted in a fractured skull and was at the time life-threatening.

But from someone who saw the crash, in a letter to Norman Parker, who had become Graham's friend, an account of what happened is revealed graphically for the first time.

Dated 18 January the letter reports that it was in Event 15, billed as the Palmerston Handicap, a 'Novelty' race. Graham was the back marker at 150 yards. On 90 yards was a B. McGee, E. Pinker was on 50 yards and M. Reid on 'Lt' – presumably scratch.

The letter describes how Graham had won his first two starts and was 'riding really well, but was beaten by Peter Pollett in his third start.

'He came out to ride in the first handicap race and was on 150 yards. Boy did he go! Probably determined to make up for his defeat in the previous race. Well, he took off and

Graham proudly carries the flag as captain of Australia on the grand parade before the final Test at Wembley in 1950. Behind him at far left Aub Lawson, Ken LeBreton, Vic Duggan, Jack Young and Arthur Payne.

Graham was all-action . . . and perfectly balanced. Birmingham's 1949 First Division league placing was next to last but his personal points total was only just topped by England number one Jack Parker at Belle Vue.

Birmingham team mates get together at the 1952 Wembley World Final: Arthur Payne (left), Dan Forsberg and Graham.

at the pit bend was really flying, picked up 50 yards on the back straight and, coming into the top bend, was 20 yards behind Pinker when Pinker fell.

'Graham, coming round very fast, either touched him with his footrest or else in trying to avoid Pinker he lost control. All I saw was Pinker on the ground then next thing Graham shot over his handlebars and went sliding along the track on his face and stomach, arms trailing at his sides just like a wooden soldier. And he just stopped and never moved.

'The crowd (10,000) had first stood for two minutes in memory of Ken [*LeBreton who had died on 5 January in a crash at the Sydney Sports Ground*] who was the idol of the Palmerston North crowds and, believe me, that same crowd was silent for a long time after the ambulance had left with Graham.

'I am fully confident he will be OK, being young and strong. I guess he can take it.'

Earlier in the letter it is said that permission to see Graham in hospital had been refused because he was 'still dangerously ill, but showing slight improvement.'

In a copy of the programme for the meeting by Event 15 in Graham's hand he has written in red ink '*Fractured my skull*' and there is a cross by his name and Pinker's.

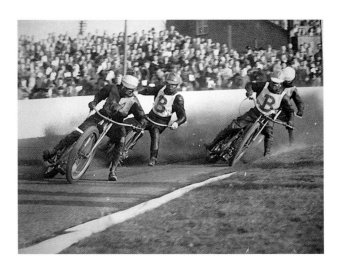

Far left: Action from Perry Barr; Jack Biggs out in front of Graham and Eric Boothroyd, with Cliff Watson just behind.

Left: Pushing pedals when the fast life had ended: Graham, the natural athlete and born racer, was still competing in cycling road races well into his fifties.

Commentator E.W. Sullivan, reviewing the New Zealand season in the World Edition of the 1951 *Stenner's Speedway Annual*, wrote: 'In my opinion these handicaps must go. Too many of the inexperienced are falling and involving the "Big Boys" in accidents. Graham Warren was another sufferer at Palmerston North.'

Just how much is revealed by Graham's son Mark, who says: 'While Graham was in a coma he had vivid dreams of Ken LeBreton, they were quite good friends. When Graham woke up he was very disorientated, he thought Ken was on the mend and still alive. It took him several months before he could sign his own name correctly! And a while to do it at his own wedding soon after the crash.

'It wasn't until he won the Midland Riders Championship in 1953 that he started to feel anything like he was before.'

Among the souvenirs: Graham towards the end of his life with one of his World Final race jackets.

Chapter 25
SPEEDWAY'S CHAMPION THUNDER-STEALER

INTRODUCING the champion thunder-stealer of the speedways, Archie Windmill, the man with the longest left leg in the sport, who was convinced his name will be on the Hackney track record for ever.

He also knew how Danish hard man Morian Hansen came to be pursued by a gunman, why Doug Wells had to see an ambulance and what happened to Split Waterman's false teeth.

One of the great things about being in the company of Archie Windmill was that the lady in his life, the lovely Sonia, made the most exceedingly good sausage rolls.

The other thing was that, as he approached his nineties, Archie was not only still going strong, but he – and Sonia – knew how to enjoy life and live it every day to the full. One of their particular delights was a cruise round Alaska.

And when the 2002 President-Elect of the Veteran Speedway Riders Association, Geoff Pymar, died just before being invested with the chain of office, Archie, who had been VSRA President in 2001, cheerfully soldiered on, stumping the country to carry out his presidential duties for a further twelve months.

And loving every minute of it.

WINDMILL, ARCH: *Born Watford 1914. Rode on the grass at Barnet in 1934 and made his speedway debut at Birmingham two years later. Within a few weeks he was signed by Hackney Wick where he partnered the famous American Cordy Milne. Arch remained at Hackney until 1939 and then served six years in the RAF. On demobilisation he joined Wimbledon and covered himself with glory at the opening meeting at Wembley in 1947 when he scored a brilliant 11 points to help Wimbledon win an exciting match by one point. Was transferred to Walthamstow soon after the start of the 1949 season.*

The start of it all, an early ride at the Barnet grass track: Even then Archie, No.6 on the inside, had a leg that seemed too long for the bike.

Above left: *The smooth operator on the inside track at Barnet: Archie on his way to the final – 'because that's where the money was'.*

Above right: *A tall tale from Archie (standing) for his Hackney team mates. From left they are Charlie Appleby (in the doorway), Tommy Bateman having a crafty drag, Stan Dell and, facing away, Doug Wells. The interloper is Max Grosskreutz, then promoting and riding at Norwich, who is behind Tommy Bateman.*

But that's only part of the story. A mere 19-line entry, in a publication entitled *Who's Who In Speedway* compiled by journalist Tom (Seven Treacle Puddings) Morgan *(see page 108)*, does scant justice to the endearing and colourful character of Arch Windmill.

The booklet, costing one-shilling-and-sixpence – or 7.5p in today's money – was published by the organisation of which *Speedway Echo* was the flagship, a magazine edited in its early days by the redoubtable Mr Morgan, whose other hats included that of 'Broadsider' of the *Sunday People* and Speedway Reporter for the *News Chronicle*. It being a time when national daily and Sunday newspapers enjoyed the luxury of having speedway correspondents on their sporting editorial staff.

In reality a very slim paperback, the advertisements for *Who's Who In Speedway* were a trifle misleading, showing as they did an apparently very fat volume similar in dimensions to that rather weightier other *Who's Who* with the distinctive red dust jacket.

It is a mere professional blip, of course, but Broadsider Morgan got Archie's birth date wrong. It was 5 June, 1915.

However, from the fact that Mr Morgan saw fit to highlight in his tome an 11-point return by Archie for Wimbledon against Wembley, you will deduce that the Windmill name did not appear regularly alongside those of the high scoring glamour boys who were the star performers of the day.

Your deduction would be – as Sherlock the master detective was so fond of saying – elementary. But we will deal with how that particular incident came to be recorded for posterity in the annals of the cinders sport in a little while.

For Archie will readily admit that he was never a star name, never, for instance, a top flight heat leader or a regular international and certainly never a World Finalist. The best that he did in pursuit of the world title was to reach the second round in 1949 and 1950 and the first round in 1952.

But he knew, and rode with the best. Morian Hansen, for instance, who had a hard man image.

According to Archie: 'Morian was a nice enough bloke, and he didn't want trouble with people. I remember when I was at Hackney they brought over another countryman of his, Balthzar Hansen. Fred Evans, the manager, brought him over and originally the idea was to pair them together – good publicity, wasn't it?

'Anyway, Balthzar couldn't speak a word of English, but they fixed him up with an old car and after a little while he had an accident in Hackney High Road. He hit a milk float. The police couldn't make head nor tale of things, so they sent for Morian to interpret for him. And Morian said all the wrong things – made it look as though it was all Balthzar's fault. And Balthzar spent a night in the cells.

'Well, you can imagine the pantomime at the police station with Balthzar not being able to speak English. When he got out, Balthzar was stalking round the stadium with a gun and he was going to shoot Morian – so that pairing never came about. They daren't put them together.

'But Morian was hard on the track. One night during a race he had trouble with the bike. It upset him a bit and when he came in – I've never seen it done before – he got hold of the bike by the tube below the saddle and the front forks, lifted it above his head and threw it against the pit wall.'

Archie started riding at the old Barnet grass track, with the likes of George Wilks, Bob

Wells and Tommy Price, men who were to become stars with Wembley. Tommy became England's first World Champion in 1949.

Archie says: 'They used to get round. But George and I used to go for the final because that's where the money was. You got a bit of start money, but no prize money. It was the semi-finals and the finals where you got the money. I was working in a garage. So was George. He was on motorbikes in the garage, but our wages weren't enough to pay for our transport to get to all the places where we wanted to race.

'We built a lot of our bikes in the back of the garage. I did Cordy Milne's bike in there.'

The Milne brothers, Jack and Cordy *(see page 80)*, from America, were sensational new arrivals in Britain in 1936. Jack went on to win the world title the following year, and Cordy was favourite for the championship when war caused the World Final to be called off in 1939. There are few people around now who had first-hand contact with the Milnes.

Archie says: 'Cordy was so dedicated. He admitted to me that "in races that I want to win, I can't help you." He never got the World Championship, which was what he really wanted. What he used to do – I didn't mind in a way – but he used to take the best positions at the gate. He always took the inside. But I didn't mind because once or twice when we were on two and four, he'd take two and I'd take four and I got out of the gate first.

'He couldn't help it – he was just that sort of bloke. Now Jack was different. Jack was more laid back than Cordy. Jack could afford to be more laid back because he knew he was good. Cordy wanted only to win.

'But Jack wasn't like that. He was modest. And he'd never tell you he was World Champion. Jack was also dedicated. He would practise all the time. I'd turn up at New Cross and he'd be practising starts in the car park before a meeting. And that was his secret. He'd go to the starting line and – bump. He was gone.

'Cordy was a little bit of a wild man. He'd take you out to the fence if you were in his way, whether you were his team partner or not.

'We were at Belle Vue one night, and Cordy Milne had upset Frank Varey. I was standing there with Cordy, and Frank came up and said: "Milney, I'm going to 'do' you tonight." I thought it was a bit of a joke. But he must have been serious because we came off the line and I'm the meat in the sandwich. We go into the first bend and Varey comes off the fence and hits Cordy and I finish up in a heap on the ground and I had nothing to do with it. But I got excluded. They said it was my fault.

'Cordy used to put his bike into the workshops at Harringay or Hackney, and it cost him the earth. What used to happen was that with a rider like Cordy who was competing in top class league racing, his motors had to be absolutely reliable. So the stadium mechanics used to slap in all new stuff – and it was costing him a lot of money.

'When we did bikes, we'd have a look at the crank pin, and if it could do another meeting we'd let it go. If a piston barrel wasn't too bad, we'd let that go. The mechanics at the stadiums wouldn't risk it.

'If the stadium did your bike, you got a bill for the work time – the hours – and then a bill for every item. Harringay never had a good workshop before the war because there was nobody in charge of it like there was after the war when Wal Phillips *(see page 123)* took over. He got it properly equipped because he knew about engines. If you had an engine done by Wal, you had a goer.

'The week before that famous night at Wembley I was going down the back straight at Wimbledon and my motor blew. The con rod broke. Jack Parker *(see page 30)* was there and said to me that he was going over to the JAP engine factory at Tottenham.

'So I went with him and they told Jack: "We've developed a new short stroke motor (because the engines in use then were long stroke) and it's come up well on the test bed, but nobody's ridden it."

'And Jack said: "No, I can't risk it. I'll have the standard engine."

'When it came to me I thought to myself: I've got nothing to lose, have I? So I said I'd have it. I put it in for Wembley and I went past Bill Kitchen as though he was standing still. I went past all of them. And in the pits there was a real to-do. They thought I'd got an oversized motor, you see.

'They were all on about it.

'Do what you like, I told them, but I've just got the engine from JAPs – it's a new short stroke. I'd had a lovely time. But the next week, they'd all got them. And it was a different story then.'

Archie's night of magic at Wembley is the stuff of legend. In a *Speedway Gazette* series, *My Greatest Thrill*, it was headlined *One Hour of Glory*, and was featured in a marvellous

*It's that leg again:
Archie gets into a bit
of a tangle with Joe
Abbott, then
Harringay captain.*

little cameo called *Out Of The Blue*, which reported the drama like this:

'*ARCH WINDMILL, long-legged, poker-faced reserve rider, is champion thunder stealer of the speedways. Arch excelled himself at Wembley's opening meeting when he scored 11 points, and not only saved Wimbledon from almost certain defeat, but won the match for them. In his first ride he beat Bill Kitchen, and in his three subsequent races figured in 5-1 wins for the fighting Dons, partnered twice by Norman Parker and once by Lloyd Goffe. Arch was virtually unbeaten, for the only man who passed him was his captain, Parker . . . '*

Wimbledon were trailing by eight points with three races to go, and Archie said at the time: 'I was down to ride in Heats 12 and 13 and to say that I was feeling jittery would be putting it mildly. It was a warm evening, but I found myself shivering. The Empire Stadium can make you feel that way on ordinary occasions.'

Only those around at the time can understand, but the Wembley crowds of those days topped 60,000 and more every week. Archie's jitters are therefore understandable because, he revealed, out there on the track Wembley captain Bill Kitchen told him: 'There are 90,000 here tonight.'

Archie takes up the story again: 'I had shaken everybody, including myself, by beating Bill Kitchen in Heat 4. In my second outing, Heat 9, I had figured in a 5-1 win with Norman Parker. In Heat 12 Norman and I got another 5-1 and we reduced Wembley's lead to four points, but I still had that sinking feeling in the pit of my stomach.

'I went to the starting gate for Heat 13 with my team mate Lloyd Goffe, who had injured a wrist. Split Waterman was our main opposition, and I said to myself: "Well, it's now or never, Arch, old son."

'And we did it! Another 5-1 and we were level 39-39.'

Archie's task was done – with one heat to go. But there was more drama to come. And the Dons pair of Cyril Brine and Dick Harris had to take on Wembley's Bob Wells, Archie's old Barnet grass track mate, and Bronco Wilson. It was still anybody's match.

Bob Wells fell at the first bend and Dick Harris was excluded when he crossed the white line, leaving Cyril Brine to battle it out with Bronco Wilson. Brine held off the Wilson challenge to clinch a one point win for Wimbledon.

I'm no world beater' Archie is reported as saying, 'and may never again rise to the heights of that May evening at Wembley, but I'll never experience a greater thrill than the winning of that match by the Dons.'

Archie again: 'Actually, a lot of the big boys used to come down to that Barnet grass track. Eric Chitty used to go there and Lionel Van Praag. I got friendly with Praagy. You couldn't talk to him about personal things. But talk to him about bikes and you were there. He was all right.

'We used to ride on Sundays of course. I rode a Rudge then, and this one Sunday he said: "Look, I've got an engine up at the stadium at Wembley. I used it in the London Riders Championship. It's getting on but it's not bad. If you'd like to you can borrow that."

'Well, I flew up there to Wembley and got it and I won the Southern Area Championship on it. And that's how I got to Hackney. When you won the Southern Area Championship you automatically got a contract with a London speedway track. You didn't have a choice. I had to go to Hackney.

'In between riding on the grass I went up to Birmingham, to Hall Green. Someone had said to me that they were short of riders there and I could get a ride. Billy Dallison was team captain there and he was more or less selecting. He said to me: "I'd love to put you in, but you haven't really got the right equipment or the experience."

'My equipment wasn't up to scratch. I'd got an old style hub on the back wheel, the old style frame and the forks had got a brake on for grass track. It was much too heavy and cumbersome.

'Then this Hackney business came along and I went to see Fred Evans. I thought I'd be doing a few second halves, but Fred said to me: "You're in the team."

'Well, I hadn't got a clue, had I? I knew nothing about team racing. And in my first race at Hackney they all went into the first bend flat out – well, on the grass I'd never done that. Anyway, I soon dropped into it and I did all right and stayed with Hackney until the war.

'At that time Hackney were First Division, but in 1938 they wanted to run on a Saturday night – the same night as Harringay. Harringay complained and said they'd be taking their crowd. So Hackney said: "That's it, we'll go Second Division." And that was a good move because the crowds were dropping off a little bit.

'But we'd got some good riders. There was Frank Hodgson, myself, Jim Baylais, Doug Wells, Stan Dell, Charlie Appleby was there. Where Fred Evans was clever, really, he got us in the dressing room and said: "Now look, sort out yourselves. I don't want to make up pairings – you sort out your pairings yourself. I went with Stan Dell who was a leg trailer, I was foot-forward, and it worked. We took off.'

Hackney won the league championship that year in 1938. Hackney and Norwich had identical records Played 16 Won 12 Drawn 0 Lost 4 Points 24. *Speedway News* finished its weekly publication before all the league matches had been completed and readers had to wait until the first *Winter Bulletin* in December to learn that Hackney had won the title on

Archie joins the 'top boys' in the 1947 Wimbledon team: Standing from the left Dick Harris, Mike Erskine, Archie, Lloyd Goffe, Cyril Brine. Sitting promoter Ronnie Greene, Les Wotton, Norman Parker, George Saunders and chief mechanic Bert Dixon.

The Walthamstow offer in 1949 was an offer Archie couldn't refuse. They were Charlie May, manager John Deeley, Jim Boyd, Benny King, Bill Osbourne, Harry Edwards and Reg Reeves. Archie is lurking between John Deeley and Jim Boyd. Dick Geary is on the bike.

superior race points.

Carry on, Archie: 'One thing that happened to me at Hackney, they'd had one or two record attempts by Eric Chitty and Malcolm Craven *(see page 142)*. Then I went out for my first league race – and it was one of those nights when everything goes well and I broke the four lap record.

'Then came the war, the track was bombed, when they started up again the track was a different size, so I've got the Hackney four lap record for ever.

'When it comes to starting, some riders of course prefer the outside positions. What they used to do at Hackney – the visitors didn't know this – they put a lot of dirt on the outside for Dicky Case. And Dicky used to go flat out round the outside – he never shut down. If someone was in his way he'd go through them. The visitors didn't know the outside had been doctored for Dicky, but I did. If they said to me: "Sorry, mate, you've got gate number four", I didn't mind. I'd say: "Thank you very much".

'I used to travel to meetings with Doug Wells. The first time he gave me a lift in his car we were going to Newcastle. We got there and he drove straight past the track. I said: "What's going on Doug? The track's over there. We just passed it."

'He said: "I must see an ambulance." And whenever he went to a meeting he had to see an ambulance somewhere. It was a superstition.

'Frank Hodgson wouldn't go out on the track first. He wanted to be last out. Now me, I had a blue pullover my mother gave me when I started grass track racing, and I wore it on the grass. I never got into any trouble, so I thought that was my lucky jumper and I wore it all the time – even on hot summer nights, I still wore it.

'It got dumped in the end with my leathers. But they all had something like that. I'm left-handed, so I'd always put on my left-hand glove first. I wouldn't put the right-hand one on first – and if I made a mistake I got worried. If throttles had been on the left-hand side, I reckon I'd have been better still.

'One time at Wimbledon I was racing against Split Waterman *(see page 95)* and I saw him down on his hands and knees scrabbling around on the track. After the race I stopped and said: "Split, what's going on?" He said: "I've lost my false teeth and I'm taking a bit of crumpet out tonight." So I got off the bike and we were both scrabbling about down there looking for his false teeth.

'By this time the track staff are coming over to find out what's going on. Well, we couldn't tell them what we were really after. So he said: "Tell them I've lost my watch strap." The story got out and they had women writing in to the track saying if Split couldn't tell the time they had a watch he could have. He was quite a lad with the ladies. Him and Bruce Abernethy.

'You know, that's what's wrong with speedway today? We never used to go home straight after a meeting, we'd all go up into the club and mix with the supporters. And they don't do that today. I mean, supporters pay their money and that's money for us, the riders.

'After the war they wanted to balance the teams and so they pooled the riders. I was allocated to Wimbledon. I wanted to go to Wembley because it was nearer home and I knew most of them there. But you didn't have a choice.

'Now Wimbledon had a good bunch of riders – all triers. But Ronnie Greene should have let Norman Parker *(see page 40)* pick the team – yet for some reason he wouldn't let him do that. When it came to the pairings, Ronnie did it all wrong.

'I was partnered with Smiler (Les) Wotton. He rode the line like me. If I'd been put with George Saunders or Lloyd Goffe or Mike Erskine, it would have worked. Ronnie Greene also put me with Norman, and we used to get in each other's way.

'Wimbledon did very well, considering, but that team could have done a lot better. At Wembley, old Bill Kitchen was the one who sorted them out. Alec Jackson, the manager, appreciated that Bill Kitchen knew what he was talking about and they had a wonderful team for a while.

'At Wimbledon, they didn't like anyone to beat Norman. And at West Ham, they didn't like anyone to beat Eric Chitty. It wasn't Norman. He didn't mind. But they want to see the captain at the top, don't they? It's only natural. Occasionally of course I was a bad boy and beat him. I will say this, though, he could beat me a lot more times than I could beat him.

'But as soon as I beat him, straight away – reserve. They demoted me. But after my magic night at Wembley, Ronnie Greene said to me: "You're in the team for the rest of the year."

'Of course, riders don't perform the same every week. And if you blew a motor, well you were out for the rest of the night. At Wimbledon they had one spare bike and I couldn't have that. They saved that for Norman. Well, you couldn't have him out. We didn't have spare bikes in those days. Blokes took spare engines, but we didn't have spare bikes.

'To give you some idea of the money in those days: at Hackney, before the war, I was knocking up between £80 and £100 a week (equivalent to around £2,800). It doesn't sound much now but the ordinary working man then was getting £7.10s (equivalent to about £240), it was good money.'

'In speedway, in those days, we were all good friends really. What we used to do at Hackney, we'd look down the programme and see who had had a bad night. And we'd say: "OK. Well you're going to win a couple of races in the second half to make up for it."'

The President and his lady: Archie with the World Speedway Riders Association Presidential chain of office he wore in 2001 and 2002, and the lovely Sonia.

Though a 'full time' speedway rider, after the war Archie ran a garage business, but was the victim of a financial disaster brought about by an associate who let him down and lost him nearly all his money.

'I'd come in late after riding, and sometimes work all night in the garage. I was doing well, and things were going nicely. I'd invested my pre-war racing winnings in the business, and if he had played the game we could both have had a nice little earner. But it all went. After that you don't come up again.

'I left Wimbledon, where it was big time, and I was riding against the top boys, because I was coming to the end of my time, really. And to be honest, I didn't like Ronnie Greene too much. And Walthamstow made me a good offer.'

One of the 'top boys' of the time was Vic Duggan, who had returned sensationally to post-war Britain in 1947 and been virtually unbeatable – due not only to his ability, but to an advanced lightweight frame design.

Archie says: 'Vic would never lend his bike to other people. But one night, he'd had a good night at Halifax and he said to me in the second half: "Have a go on mine."

'Cor, bloody hell. It was like a feather. Compared with the old Rudge that I had. Until I made my own. Because of my long legs I made a complete new frame – and it was done on my sitting room floor. I did well on that. Then George Greenwood, who was running a spares shop for Alec Jackson gave me an order for six.

'I didn't patent it or anything. Then the next thing I know, Excelsior are building it. I was a bit put out about it because I had high hopes of that. Here, Sonia commented: "He was a hopeless businessman, hopeless . . ."

'My long legs . . . well I went into a turn at Harringay one night and my handlebars went down the top of my boot. I hung three of us on the fence – couldn't help it, old Joe Abbott was one. So what we did, we cut the forks and brought the head of the bike up higher and it worked all right.'

Archie's career finally came to an end at Southern League Aldershot. What made him decide that was it?

Archie says: 'Well, you just get a feeling you've had enough, and I'd had enough. I was thirty-eight and I wanted to pack up while I could still win races – and that's what I did. I was hoping to start another business, but I hadn't got the money. So I had to go to work, and I thought that if I didn't do something then I'd be too old to get a decent job. I hadn't got enough money to start a business again, but a friend of mine had a tyres business in Watford – I'd worked for him before the war – and I went back to him.

'I was quite happy doing that, but I'd have been happier if it had been mine. I'm not complaining. I've still got my health. Some of them have not been so lucky. I'll be honest with you, I would have loved to have thrown caution to the winds and got more than I did. But I weighted it up and I thought: "Your luck's going to run out."

'Yes, of course I had ambitions to be a World Champion, and I had my chances. But look at (Jack) Parker – he never won a World Championship.

'You know, people still come up to me and tell me they remember me at Wimbledon all those years ago. Some even tell me that I was their Mum's hero.'

Archie died aged ninety-two in 2007.